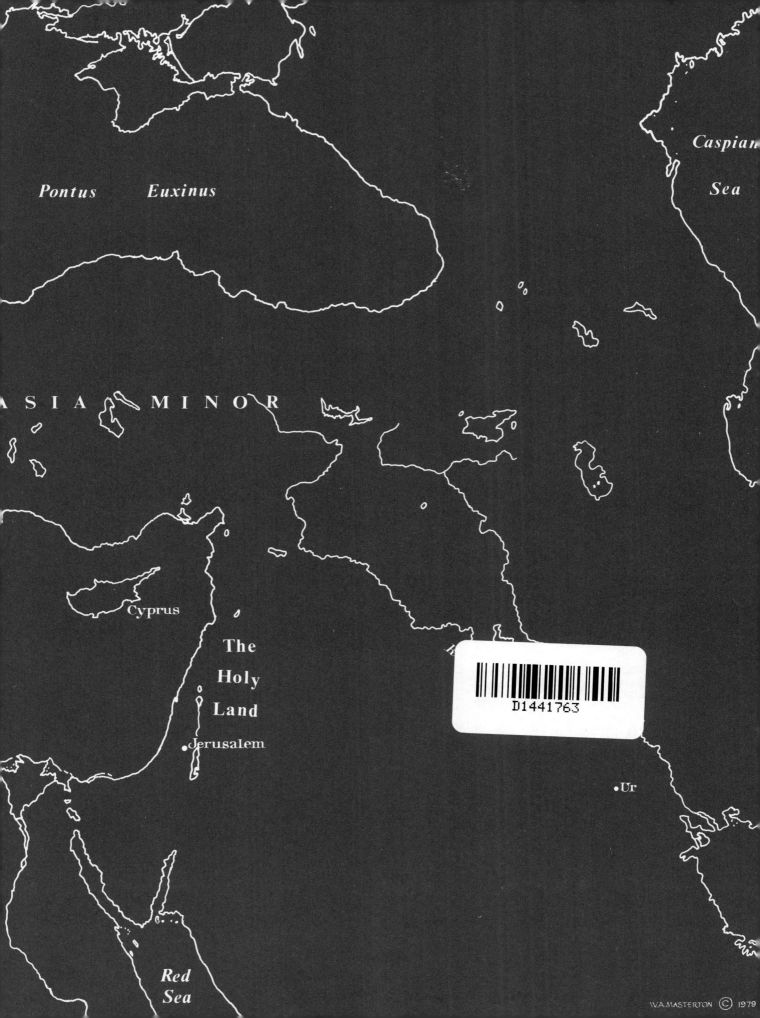

Pontus Euxinus

Caspian Sea

ASIA MINOR

Cyprus

The
Holy
Land

•Jerusalem

•Ur

Red
Sea

W.A.MASTERTON © 1979

THE BIBLE IN FOCUS

THE BIBLE

Donors Inc

IN FOCUS

A pictorial of prophecies, people and places

Compiled by Clem Clack
in association with Dawn Saward and Olive Clack

First published 1980
Second Printing 1981
Donors Inc
PO Box 65
Blackburn South 3130
Victoria Australia

© copyright Clem Clack 1980

Wholly designed and typeset in Australia
Printed in Hong Kong

National Library of Australia
Cataloguing-in-publication data

Clack, Clem.
   The Bible in focus.
   Index.
   Index.
   Bibliography.
   ISBN 0 908250 00 2

1. Bible — Geography. I. Saward, Dawn,
joint author. II. Clack, Olive, joint
author. III. Title.

220. 9'1

Acknowledgements
Acknowledgement and thanks are due to the
following persons and organizations for their
kind co-operation.

Script readers and advisors
W. Griffith, for detailed editing of script
T. Alec Mairs and Brian Clack
Colin McKenzie
Rev. Euan Fry
Gordon G. Garner B.A. B.D.

Typing
Edith Grey and Janet Stebbins

Art Work
Ed. Bently, of Wycliffe Bible Translators,
page 65
Bruce Walker
W. A. Masterton, for preparing maps for end
papers and the Bible Lands of planet earth
Miss F. Willis, Christian Book Room Hong
Kong, for her kind permission to use illumi-
nated texts

Others
Christian Enterprises for their prayerful and
practical support
Numerous friends for their helpful contribu-
tions
Scripture quotations are taken from:
The Authorised Version,
The Revised Standard Version. Copyright ©
1946,
Division of Christian Education of the National
Council of Churches of Christ in the United
States of America,
Verses marked TLB are taken from the Living
Bible. Copyright © 1971 by Tyndale House
Publishers, Wheaton Ill. Used by permission,
The Modern Language Bible, MLB, the New
Berkeley Version. Copyright © 1969 Zonder-
van Publishing house, used by permision,
And on occasions free translations and ab-
ridged paraphrasing.

Bibliography
Buried History. Magazine published by The
Australian Institute of Archaeology, and es-
pecially the articles by Dr Colin J. Hemer on
the seven churches of Revelation
Donald Grey Barnhouse, *Genesis*
J. Sidlow Baxter, *Explore the Book*
Philip Teng, *Christ seeks Asia, lectures on
Revelation,*
Halley's *Bible Hand Book*
H. C. Hewlett, *The Glories of our Lord*
Henrietta C. Mears, *What the Bible is all About*
J. Oswald Sanders, *Christ Incomparable*
Wilbur M. Smith, *Egypt in Prophecy*
C. W. Sleming, *Bible Digest*
G. Campbell Morgan, *The Gospel according to
Mark*

Information and thoughts have been gleaned
from numerous books and magazines over the
past thirty years; some authors' names and the
source of some articles have not been kept. A
partial bibliography is listed above.

Photo Credits
The Australian Institute of Archaeology 10,
   22, 68LoL, 108T
Rupert Bishop 32LoR, 78, 119Lo, 153Lo
Werner Braun 30R, 33T, 34LoL, 35LoR, 37,
   39R, 45, 48T, 70Lo, 92Lo, 100LoR
Joan Carson 102CL
Jeff Clack 24L, 31LoR, 34TL, 35L, 38L, 40,
   43, 50T, 52T, 64T, 84LoL, 111T, 112Lo,
   113T, 141TR, 143CR, 146CL, 152Lo, 158
Peter Crespin 125T
Jack Cupper 32L, 44TL, 54C, 59L, 94T, 102T
Custodians of Jacob's Well 87T
The Government of Cyprus 125Lo
Dr Morris C. Davis 20L, 131Lo
The Government of Greece 41, 50L, 58, 85T,
   126, 128, 130LoR, 131T, 132Lo, 134TL,
   138L, 143LoL
Holy Land Hotel, Jerusalem. To the manage-
   ment, for permission to photograph their
   excellent model of the Jerusalem of 2000
   years ago
Heather Howey 102CLo
Honey Board 83Lo
Japheth Press 90 Map
Keith Graham 141C
Rev T. Keyte 26Lo
K. O. Kinney 102CR
Mr Paul Kitchen MBBS, FRACS 25T, 29Lo,
   56T, 117C
W. Lennox 86Lo
Matson Photo Service. Mr and Mrs Eric Matson
   Los Angeles 96TL, 108C
Earle Meager 139Lo
Rolf Meier 103LoR, 154LoR
Garo H. Nalbandian 11, 15Lo, 18, 20T, 36Lo,
   46, 52, 57L, 60L, 61L, 67LoL, 71T, 71LoL,
   72/73, 75TR, 75Lo, 79T, 80, 81TR, 81Lo,
   82T, 84L, 89T, 91Lo, 97T, 98, 103LoL,
   103T, 104T, 106Lo, 107Lo, 110, 112C,
   114TL, 114LoR, 115TR, 115LoR, 120/
   121, 122, 123C, 127, 153TR, 154LoL
E. C. Pope 141T
Robert Stokes 9TL, 9CL, 14C, 33Lo, 111Lo
Robyn Schuller's Portrait 54R
The Government of Turkey 133, 140, 137T
Dr V. Wilson 51T, 93T
Bill Wood 153TL
Yossi Eshbol 155TR, 155TL
The remaining 230 photographs were taken
by the authors.

Contents

GOD'S PROMISES TO ABRAHAM, ISAAC AND JACOB

In the book of Genesis, chapters 12 to 25 are devoted to the story of Abraham, and only chapters 1 and 2 to the story of creation. God places the emphasis, not on cosmic origins, but on one speck of humanity, through whom He would ultimately bless all of mankind. It takes only eleven chapters to relate the events of the first 2000 years of bible history, and 918 chapters to tell of the events of the next 2000 years which commenced with the story of Abraham and his descendants. This makes Genesis 12 the Great Divide of Old Testament history.

Note the inclusiveness of the promises made by God to Abraham about 4000 years ago.
I will bless thee — the individual
I will make thy name great — the family
I will make of thee a great nation — the nation
In thee shall all the families of the earth be blessed — the world   Genesis 12: 2-3

A section of the Jezreel Valley as seen from the slopes of Mount Tabor

6

A PEOPLE AND A LAND FOREVER

Arise, walk through the

The Lord your God is bringing you into a good land, a land of brooks of water . . . a land of wheat and barley, of vines and fig trees and pomegranates; a land of olive trees and honey . . . a land whose stones are iron, and out of whose hills you can dig copper.   Deuteronomy 8: 7-9

A section of the Jezreel Valley viewed from Megiddo

The source of the brook in the photograph below is a spring in Mount Hermon and flows into the Jordan River. It has done so for thousands of years. The Bible says: *'The cold flowing streams from the crags of Mount Hermon never run dry. These can be counted on, but not my people.'*   TLB Jeremiah 18: 14, 15

length and the breadth of the land Genesis 13:17

Israel's copper mining area

A land whose stones are iron

9

I AM THE LORD who brought you from Ur

Reconstructed ziggurat in Ur on the Euphrates River, Iraq

The Lord had said to Abraham: 'Go from your country and your father's house to the land that I will show you and I will make of you a great nation'... So Abraham went as the Lord had told him.   Genesis 12: 1-4

It is quite possible that Abraham lived in a comfortable two-storied home in Ur when God called him to become a tent dweller. No man has ever lost anything by giving up something for God. Ur, of the Chaldees, was a prosperous city for its time, with good living standards. Yet it was full of pagan and immoral practices. The ziggurat at Ur was dedicated to the moon-god.

Behind God's call to Abraham was His purpose to bless man. Neither man's sin and failure, nor his subsequent breaking of God's holy laws, could alter that purpose. God called Abraham to leave much, but promised him more. Faith that truly believes God, is a faith that obeys God. Abraham's confidence was his conviction that his God was able to perform all that He had promised.

Excavated ziggurat

An Iraqi policeman on the steps of the ziggurat

to give you this land to possess Genesis 15:7

And Abraham dwelt at Hebron.   Genesis 13: 18

God said to Abraham: '*I will give to you, and to your descendants after you, the land of your sojournings, all the land of Canaan, for an everlasting possession.*'
Genesis 17: 8

God chose a people:
In whom He could display His grace to mankind.
To whom He could entrust the Holy Scriptures.
By whom He could witness to other nations.
Through whom the promised Messiah would come.

Ishmael is born

Some Arabs and desert dwellers today are possible descendants of Ishmael.

Right: Market Day in Beersheba

Abraham's wife, Sarah, took Hagar the Egyptian, her maid, and gave her to Abraham her husband as a wife. Abraham called the name of his son, whom Hagar bore, Ishmael. Genesis 16: 3, 15

Abraham and Sarah had been in the promised land for ten years, and because Sarah was beyond the age of child bearing, their faith wavered although God had promised seed as the *stars of heaven.*
see Genesis 15: 5

His word was better than any birth certificate. In her impatience, Sarah tried to help God by human means in giving her maid to Abraham.

A name is changed

Abraham's name was originally Abram, however, God added the letter H, which is formed by breathing out. God's breath of life to Abraham brought fruitfulness. When he was an old man of ninety-nine years, his son Isaac was born. Abraham means, *Father of the multitude.* see Genesis 17: 5

Abraham dug a well and called the place Beer-sheba which means either 'the well of the seven,' or 'well of the oath'. A number of ancient wells exist in the area, including one over 43 metres (140 feet) deep dating from about 1200 B.C. Beersheba has become a thriving city since Israel became a nation in 1948.

Upper left: An ancient well at Beersheba

Abraham planted a tamarisk tree as a token of God's goodness.   Genesis 21: 33

Abraham was a tent dweller. Bedouin tents are a common sight in the desert areas even today. Whenever the patriarchs settled for a time, they did three things:
- Built an altar.
- Pitched a tent.
- Dug a well.

In their old age Abraham and Sarah had a son, they called him Isaac
Genesis 21:2, 3

After these things God tested Abraham . . . and said: *'Take your only son Isaac, whom you love, and go to the land of Moriah and offer him there as a burnt offering upon one of the mountains of which I shall tell you.'* Genesis 22: 1-2

Abraham provided the wood,
the fire and
the knife.
God provided the sacrifice. When Abraham was about to plunge the knife into his son, God said: 'Stop.' Abraham looked and saw a ram caught in a thicket of thorns. Two thousand years later, Jesus Christ, with His head in a crown of thorns, became the Lamb of God's providing. He died on that same mount.

My son, God will provide himself the lamb. Genesis 22: 8

A bride for Isaac.
Abraham sent his servant back to the country of his birth to choose a wife for Isaac. Rebekah came out to draw water. She was a beautiful girl. Abraham's servant had asked God for a sign, and in answer to his prayer, Rebekah offered water to him and his camels. That night the servant stayed at the home of Rebekah's parents, and Laban her brother said: *'Rebekah is before you, take her and go, and let her be the wife of your master's son, as the Lord had spoken.'* Genesis 24: 51

And they called Rebekah and said to her: 'Will you go with this man?' and she said: 'I will go.' Genesis 24: 58

The servant gave Rebekah jewellery of silver and gold, and clothing . . . and Isaac lifted up his eyes and looked and behold the camels were coming . . . when Rebekah saw Isaac she got down from her camel . . . then Isaac took Rebekah into the tent and she became his wife, and Isaac loved her. Genesis 24: 53, 63-67

Isaac and Rebekah — Twins born of you shall be divided. The elder shall serve the younger Genesis 25:23

And when Rebekah's days were fulfilled twins were born. The first was born covered with reddish hair, so they called him Esau. The other was born with his hand on Esau's heel. They named him Jacob. Genesis 25: 23-26

The Lord blessed Isaac and he became rich . . . he had great possessions of flocks and herds and a great household . . . he sowed and reaped an hundredfold. Genesis 26: 12-14

When the boys grew up, Esau was a skilful hunter . . . while Jacob was a quiet man . . . when Jacob was boiling pottage, Esau came in from the field.

Esau: *'Let me eat some of that red pottage for I am famished.'*

Jacob: *'First sell me your birthright.'*

Esau: *'I am about to die, of what use is a birthright to me?'*

So Esau sold his birthright to Jacob . . . thus Esau despised his birthright. Genesis 25: 27-34

Esau forfeited the privilege of his descendants' becoming part of the line of the Messiah. When Isaac was old he called for Esau.

Isaac: *'Esau, take your quiver and bow and get me some venison, and prepare for me savoury food such as I love, that I may eat and bless you before I die.'* Genesis 27: 1-4

Jacob and Rebekah deceived Isaac by preparing savoury food. In this way, Jacob stole the blessing from his twin brother.

Esau dwelt in the hill country of Seir; Esau is Edom   Genesis 32:3

When the nation of Israel was journeying to the promised land, Esau's descendants, the Edomites, *refused to give them passageway through their territory.*   Numbers 20: 21

Thus says the Lord: 'Because Edom acted revengefully against the house of Judah . . . I will stretch out my hand against Edom . . . and I will make it a desolate wilderness.'   Ezekiel 25: 12, 13
Joel 3: 19

Esau and his descendants settled in the vicinity of this rugged area of Petra. The book of Obadiah says concerning the Edomites, *"The pride of your heart has deceived you, you who live in the clefts of the rock, whose dwelling is high, who say in your heart, 'Who will bring me down to the ground?' Though you soar aloft like the eagle, though your nest is set among the stars, thence I will bring you down,"* says the Lord.   Obadiah: 3,4

The passageway into Petra   *Right: The Treasury*

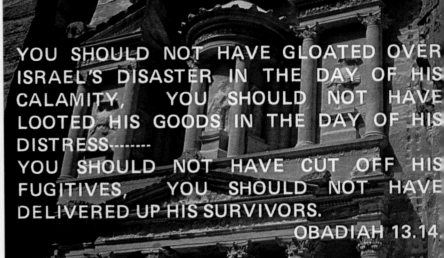

YOU SHOULD NOT HAVE GLOATED OVER ISRAEL'S DISASTER IN THE DAY OF HIS CALAMITY,   YOU SHOULD NOT HAVE LOOTED HIS GOODS IN THE DAY OF HIS DISTRESS.......
YOU SHOULD NOT HAVE CUT OFF HIS FUGITIVES,   YOU SHOULD NOT HAVE DELIVERED UP HIS SURVIVORS.

OBADIAH 13.14

PETRA — this strange city of the ancient world was rediscovered in 1812, and is now a fascinating tourist attraction. Simply by guarding the long passageway, the only entrance to Petra, the people living there were confident their city was impregnable.

Similarly, Esau's descendants thought they were unconquerable. God's judgment was declared against them because of the way they treated their kinsmen. The book of Obadiah tells the story of their downfall. When Jerusalem was being conquered by Nebuchadnezzar, King of Babylon, the Edomites came and looted the city, captured the escaping Israelites, and handed them over to their enemy. God said: *"For the violence done to your brother Jacob, shame shall cover you, and you shall be cut off for ever. You should not have gloated over his misfortune."*

Obadiah: 10,12

The Edomites faded out of existence as a nation. Some suggest that Herod the Great was the last Edomite of note.

Top: Coloured rock by the Treasury
Centre: Obelisk Tomb (above) and Bab el Siq Triclinium (below).
Bottom: Street of the Facades.

Rachel, Laban's daughter, is coming with the sheep Genesis 29:6

Isaac said to Jacob: *'You shall not marry one of the Canaanite women. Arise, go to Paddan-aram to the house of Bethuel your mother's father; and take as wife from there one of the daughters of Laban your mother's brother.'* Jacob went on his journey and met Rachel at the well. He helped her to water the sheep, then went with her to Laban. He worked with Laban and as wages he asked for Rachel to become his wife.

'So Jacob served seven years for Rachel and they seemed to him but a few days because of his love for her.' On the completion of the time, Laban deceived Jacob and gave him his elder daughter, Leah, as his wife. So Jacob served another seven years, *'then Laban gave him his daughter, Rachel, to wife.'* Genesis 28: 1, 2; 29: 20-28

A changed name for a changed person

Jacob was left alone by the brook Jabbok . . . and there wrestled a man with him until the breaking of the day . . . and he said to him: 'Your name shall no more be called Jacob but ISRAEL.'
Genesis 32: 24-28

The result of the all-night wrestling match mentioned in Genesis 32 not only brought about a change in name for Jacob, but it also transformed him from being a cunning and deceitful person to being a prince with God and with man. His descendants today are proud to call their nation by his name.

Three biological miracles were needed to commence and establish the nation of Israel. The wives of patriarchs, Abraham, Isaac, and Jacob, were childless. God intervened and accomplished these miracles. In so doing He was preparing the hearts and minds of the people for the day when the miracle of Isaiah 7: 14 would be fulfilled: *'A virgin shall conceive and bear a son.'*

The Brook Jabbok

In giving birth to her son, Benjamin, Rachel died. Jacob buried her at Bethlehem. *He set up a pillar on her grave, which is there to this day.*
Genesis 35: 18-20

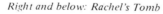

Right and below: Rachel's Tomb

From pit to prison to prime minister

Because Joseph was the favourite son of Jacob, his jealous brothers cast him into a pit, and sold him to some Midianite traders; he was taken to Egypt and sold to Potiphar, an officer of Pharaoh. *'The Lord was with Joseph and he became a successful man . . . his master saw that the Lord was with him, and the Lord caused all that he did to prosper.'* Later he was falsely accused and thrown into prison where he remained until God enabled him to interpret Pharaoh's dream concerning the years of plenty and famine. In acknowledgement Pharaoh said: *'I have set you over all the land of Egypt . . . I am Pharaoh, and without your consent no man shall lift up hand or foot in all the land of Egypt.'*

Genesis 37: 24; 39: 3; 41: 41-44

An ancient storage pit at Megiddo   Joseph was cast into a cistern type pit.

JACOB forecasts the future at family conference

Joseph was sold as a slave at seventeen years of age; at thirty he became ruler in Egypt; ten years later his father, Jacob, went to Egypt.

Jacob called together his twelve sons and said: 'Gather around me and I will tell you what is going to happen in the future.'   Genesis 49: 1

Jacob's twelve sons were founders of the twelve tribes which became the nation of Israel, the nation which has played and will play a vital role in the history of the world. Jacob's prophecies about the twelve tribes describe some remarkable events which are to happen to their descendants.

Below are two of twelve contemporary windows in a synagogue in Melbourne, Australia, depicting Jacob's prophecies to his twelve sons. The artist and designer was Dr Morris Davis.

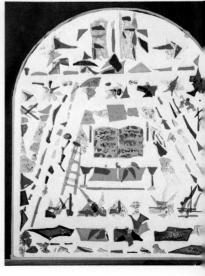

Right: 'Reuben, you are my firstborn.' The excellence of dignity and the excellence of power are represented by three strong vertical columns supporting a heavy superstructure.

Far right: 'Levi, come not thou into their secret assembly.' Levi's descendants were to be the people of the Book and the teachers of Israel. The central book in illuminated manuscript form is seen above a table with Kiddush cup. Levi's search for truth is clearly represented by an upward-directed design including a ladder to the Torah above.

All the nations came to Joseph in Egypt to buy grain, because everywhere the famine was severe Genesis 41:57

From Famine

To Plenty

God said: 'Jacob, do not be afraid to go down to Egypt, for there I will make you a great nation . . . and I will bring your descendants back again.'
Genesis 46: 3-4

Jacob and his sons and their children, a total of seventy people, went to Egypt. When Pharaoh learned they were shepherds, he permitted them to settle in the land of Goshen, where they greatly multiplied. God knew it was best that the Israelites leave Canaan, until they developed national strength; this would safeguard them against mingling and intermarrying with the idolatrous races in Canaan. Genesis 46, 47

In mercy God gave the Canaanites four hundred years to repent of their idolatry before the nation of Israel returned to the land; their idolatry included child sacrifices and gross immorality.
Genesis 15: 13-16

Centre right: Excavated ruins of the funery temple of Queen Hatshepsut at Deir el Bahri

The children of Israel settled in fertile delta country similar to this in The Nile Valley

Nation grows in spite of persecution!

Brickmaking

Now there arose a new King over Egypt who did not know Joseph. And he said to his people: 'Behold, the people of Israel are too many and too mighty for us' . . . Therefore they set task-masters over them to afflict them with heavy burdens; and they built for Pharaoh store-cities, Pithom and Raamses. The more they were oppressed, the more they multiplied. So Pharaoh the King commanded that the newborn Hebrew boys be drowned in the Nile River. Exodus 1: 8-22

MOSES IS BORN

After hiding baby Moses for three months, his mother prepared a basket of bulrushes and water-proofed it with tar and hid the baby among the reeds of the Nile. It was there that Pharaoh's daughter found, and adopted him. Exodus 2: 1-10

A section of the Nile River, Egypt

Moses was instructed in all the wisdom of the Egyptians Acts 7:22

During Israel's slavery in Egypt, God had been preparing a leader, one who had moved amongst the highest officials for forty years. Moses came as a deliverer after being himself delivered from death. He had the finest education Egypt could offer, yet his faith was centred in his mother's God, the God of Israel. This enabled him to take a race of slaves and mould them into a nation.

The plant from which papyrus is made

Right: The Egyptian figures are painted on papyrus which is made from bulrushes such as those featured above. It was probably used in the making of books in the time of Job when he said: *'Oh that my words were written! Oh that they were inscribed in a book . . . For I know that my Redeemer liveth, and He shall stand in the latter day upon the earth: and though . . . worms destroy this body, yet in my flesh I shall see God.'* Job 19: 23, 26

Such was Job's strong expression of faith in God, that he wished his words to remain for ever inscribed in a book and chiselled into rock.

MOSES lived as a prince in Pharaoh's court

Part of the ruins as seen today. The main entrance stone was 12.192 metres — 40 feet — long and weighed 150 tonnes. There are 134 huge columns; some are 24 metres — 78 feet — high, and 3.5 metres — 11½ feet — in diameter, large enough to build a room to house more than fifty people on top of each column.

The idols of Egypt shall tremble at the Lord's presence.   Isaiah 19: 1

There are approximately two hundred and fifty verses in the Old Testament which at the time they were spoken were prophecies of events yet to take place in Egypt. The areas of the Middle East that are constantly referred to in ancient Biblical prophecy are amongst the focal points of world history today, and God's plans are still being enacted on the shaky world stage.

The Egyptians shall return to the LORD and He will heal them
Isaiah 19:22 (Future prophecy)

An artist's impression of the original grandeur of the temple of Karnak, Egypt, from the 'Wonders of the Past.'

GOD called to Moses from the burning bush

Dawn breaks on Mount Moses

Moses was keeping the sheep in the mountains when he saw a strange sight; a bush burning, yet not consumed. When he turned to investigate, God called to him out of the bush: 'MOSES, MOSES!' And he said: 'Here am I.' Then God said: 'Do not come near; put off your shoes from your feet, for the place on which you are standing is holy ground.' And he said: 'I am the God of your father, the God of Abraham, the God of Isaac, and the God of Jacob.' And Moses hid his face, for he was afraid to look at God. Then the Lord said: 'I have seen the affliction of my people who are in Egypt, and have heard their cry because of their task-masters; I know their sufferings, and have come down to deliver them out of the land of the Egyptians, and to bring them up out of that land to a good and broad land, a land flowing with milk and honey. Come, I will send you to Pharaoh, that you may bring forth my people, the sons of Israel, out of Egypt.'

Exodus 3: 1-11

Let my people go   Exodus 7:16

The River Nile at Luxor

God said to Moses: 'Stand beside the river bank and meet Pharaoh there.' As Pharaoh and all his officials watched, Moses' brother Aaron, struck the water of the Nile with his rod and the river turned to blood.

Exodus 7: 15-20

Pestilence and plague cause havoc

Chortoicetes terminifera, one of the many types of locust that invade in plague proportions

The ten plagues sent by the Lord upon Egypt were:

1. Water became blood.
2. Frogs.
3. Dust became lice.
4. Flies.
5. Plague on flocks and herds so that they died.
6. Boils and sores.
7. Hail and fire.
8. Locusts.
9. Darkness.
10. Death of firstborn.   See Exodus 7-12

These plagues were not sent merely to inconvenience man or to afflict his body. They were an attack by God against the religious system of the Egyptian people. Many of the creatures, such as frogs, were sacred, and no one was permitted to kill even one.

To summarize: The Egyptians considered:

The Nile: a source of life.
Frogs: a symbol of life.
Sun and moon: givers of life.
Animals: sustainers of life.
Embalming: preparation for the next life.

The Nile River will swarm with frogs, and they will come into your houses, even into your bedrooms and into your beds! Every home in Egypt will be filled with them. They will fill your ovens and your kneading bowls; you and your people will be immersed in them. Exodus 8: 3, 4

Judgment strikes at midnight!

At midnight, the Lord smote all the firstborn in the land of Egypt.
Exodus 12: 29

The Lord said: *'Moses, speak to the congregation of Israel saying, This month shall be unto you the beginning of months . . . take every man a lamb . . . a lamb for an house, and none of you shall go out of his house until the morning. For the Lord will pass through to slay the Egyptians; and when he sees the blood on the lintel and on the two doorposts, the Lord will not allow the destroyer to enter your houses to slay you.'*
Exodus 12: 1-3, 22-23

When you come to the land which the Lord promised you, you shall keep this service. And when your children say to you: 'What do you mean by this service?' you shall say: 'It is the sacrifice of the Lord's passover, for he passed over the houses of the children of Israel in Egypt, when he slew the Egyptians but spared the children of Israel.'
Exodus 12: 25-27

And Pharaoh summoned Moses and Aaron by night, and said: 'Rise up, go forth from among my people, both you and the people of Israel; and go, serve the Lord as you have said. Take your flocks and your herds, and be gone.'
Exodus 12: 31-32

There are 90 different references in the Old Testament to God bringing the Children of Israel out of the land of Egypt. On the night of the exodus, they passed out of Africa into Asia, from slavery to freedom, from a tribal people to a nation. This is the earliest recorded instance of a great national emancipation. Their deliverance was accomplished, not by their own strategy, but by the power of God. Some victories are effected by God and man working together. This was entirely God's work.

I will sing to the LORD, He has triumphed gloriously:

THE HORSE AND HIS RIDER HATH HE THROWN INTO THE SEA. THE LORD IS MY STRENGTH AND MY SONG, AND HE HAS BECOME MY SALVATION.   Exodus 15: 1, 2

Jacob entered Egypt with his family of seventy persons. Four hundred and thirty years later they left as a nation.

Pharaoh's army pursued the children of Israel as far as the Red Sea. It was there that God caused the waters to return and they were all drowned.

Left: Abandoned boats at the Red Sea

The people found fault with Moses and said: 'Give us water to drink' . . . so Moses cried to the Lord: 'What shall I do with this people?' . . . The Lord said to Moses: 'Take the rod . . . and strike the rock at Horeb, and water shall come out.'   Exodus 17: 2-6

The Israelites ate manna (bread which the Lord supplied) *for forty years . . . until they reached the border of Canaan.*   see Exodus 16:11-35

Ain Mussa, accepted by the Moslems as the place where Moses struck the rock and the water came forth. Today the water still flows generously in an otherwise arid wilderness.

The Lord led His people through the Wilderness, for His steadfast love endures for ever.   Psalm 136: 16

28

Moses climbed the rugged mountain to meet with God, and from somewhere in the mountain God called to him and said: 'Give these instructions to the people of Israel, tell them you have seen what I did to the Egyptians, and how I brought you to myself as though on eagles' wings.'

TLB Exodus 19: 1-4

There are two mountain peaks which stand out in superb contrast: Mount Sinai and Mount Calvary; Mount Sinai, with its lightning and thunder and the rigid holy laws; Mount Calvary, where our Lord was crucified. He bore the fire and thunder of God's judgment against the law breaker, and made possible a meeting place between God and man.

Sunrise on Sinai

GOD'S BLUEPRINT FOR BETTER LIVING

The Torah

So Moses called the elders of the people, and set before them all these words which the Lord had commanded him. Exodus 19: 7

They answered: 'All that the Lord hath spoken we will do.' Exodus 19: 8

The Ten Commandments:

You shall have no other God before me.
You shall not make for yourself a graven image.
You shall not take the name of the Lord your God in vain.
Remember the Sabbath day, to keep it holy.
Honour your father and your mother.
You shall not kill.
You shall not commit adultery.
You shall not steal.
You shall not bear false witness.
You shall not covet. Exodus 20: 3-17

The first four commandments show us how we ought to live with God, the latter six show us how we ought to live with men.

It is the Jewish mother's privilege to light the Sabbath candles and recite this prayer: 'Lord of the universe, I am about to perform the sacred duty of kindling the lights in honour of the Sabbath, even as it is written: "And thou shalt call the Sabbath a delight, and the holy day of the Lord honourable" . . . Father of Mercy, O continue thy loving kindness unto me and my dear ones. Make me worthy to rear my children that they walk in the way of righteousness before Thee, loyal to Thy Law and clinging to good deeds' . . .

Teach God's laws to your children

Teach these things to your children, and talk of them when you are at home or out for a walk, at bedtime and first thing in the morning.

Deuteronomy 6: 7

You shall bind them as a sign upon your hand.

Deuteronomy 6: 8

They shall be as frontlets between your eyes.

Deuteronomy 6: 8

Write them on the doorposts of your house.

Deuteronomy 6: 9

Every law of God is right   Psalm 119:128

Only the fish with fins and scales may be eaten.
Deuteronomy 14: 9

Left: Goshawk

You may eat all clean animals. Every one that has the hoof cloven in two and chews the cud, such as oxen, sheep and goats. And the swine, because it parts the hoof but does not chew the cud, is unclean for you.   Deuteronomy 14: 3-8

You may eat all clean birds . . . you shall not eat the eagle, kite, hawk, seagull and the pelican, also many others as listed in Deuteronomy 14: 11, 20

Left: Square-tailed Kite

Left: Black Falcon

Seagull

Do not plough with an ox and a donkey harnessed together. Deuteronomy 22: 10

"Let no one be found among you . . . who practises divination or sorcery, interprets omens, engages in witchcraft, or is a medium, or spiritist, or who consults the dead. For anyone who does these things is an abomination to the Lord." Deuteronomy 18:10-12

Bring the first part of every crop to the temple, whether it be a ground crop or from fruit and olive trees. The purpose of tithing is to teach you to put God first in your lives. Nehemiah 10: 35 TLB Deuteronomy 14: 22, 23

Apples ripe for the picking

ISRAEL'S ANNUAL FESTIVALS

Seven days there shall be no leaven (yeast) *found in your houses.* Exodus 12: 19

THE PASSOVER

In the fourteenth day of the first month at even is the Lord's passover, for that was when the Lord your God brought you out of Egypt.

UNLEAVENED BREAD

Seven days you must eat unleavened bread . . . as a reminder of the bread you ate when you came out of Egypt. Leviticus 23: 5, 6
Deuteronomy 16: 1-3

The Passover Plate: from centre top, clockwise

1. The bitter herbs remind the people of the bitterness endured when they were slaves in Egypt.
2. The shank bone, a symbol of the passover lamb.
3. A mixture of grated apple, nuts and wine, a reminder of the bricks they made during their bondage.
4. Parsley, representing the hyssop used to apply the blood of the passover lamb on the door posts and the lintels.
5. Salt water, a reminder of the tears shed when in slavery in Egypt.
6. Egg, hard boiled, a type of resurrection, from the grave of Egypt to a new national life in a promised land.

After clearing from the home anything with yeast, it is disposed of by burning

The wine is partaken of four times

I WILL BRING YOU OUT

I WILL DELIVER YOU FROM BONDAGE

I WILL REDEEM YOU

I WILL TAKE YOU FOR MY PEOPLE

Christ observed the day of passover offering Himself as, *The Lamb of God who takes away the sin of the world.*
John 1: 29

Jesus took the bread and said . . . 'This is my body given for you.'
I Corinthians 11: 23, 24

The passover bread is striped and pierced. His body was striped with the scourge and pierced with the nails and the spear.

Calvary: A possible site of Christ's crucifixion

THE FESTIVAL OF FIRST FRUITS

You shall bring a sheaf of the firstfruits of your harvest unto the priest . . . he shall wave it before the Lord, on the day after the sabbath, (Sunday).
Leviticus 23: 10, 11

Christ observed the feast of firstfruits by rising from the dead on the day after the sabbath. *But now is Christ risen from the dead, and is become the firstfruits of them that slept.*
I Corinthians 15: 20

THE FESTIVAL OF PENTECOST

Leave some of the fallen grain for the poor and the stranger   Leviticus 23: 22

Pentecost was celebrated toward the end of the harvest. When Moses received the Ten Commandments, 3 000 Jews were slain. When Peter preached on the anniversary of Pentecost . . . *and the disciples were all filled with the Holy Spirit,*

Acts 2: 1-4,

3 000 Jewish souls were saved. Later, he preached to the Gentiles and ever since, there has been a mighty harvest amongst them. The Gentiles were once strangers to all of God's promises. *Now you are no longer strangers, but members of God's very own family.*   TLB Ephesians 2: 19

The two loaves offered at the festival of Pentecost were made with yeast.   Leviticus 23: 17

The two loaves are a symbol of the Jews and Gentiles being welded together in the Church of Jesus Christ. *The Gentiles are fellow heirs, members of the same body, and partakers of the promise in Jesus Christ through the Gospel.*

Ephesians 3: 6

Yeast in the Bible speaks of imperfection. As long as the Church is on earth it will never know perfection. One day the Lord Jesus *will present the church to Himself in splendour . . . holy and without blemish.*   Ephesians 5: 27

The first four Jewish festivals were fulfilled in the same chronological order at the commencement of Christianity.

PASSOVER — *Christ our Passover was sacrificed for us.*
UNLEAVENED BREAD — *This is my body given for you.*
FIRSTFRUITS — Christ the firstfruits rose on the day after the sabbath.
PENTECOST — The commencement of the great harvest of Jews and Gentiles into the Church of Jesus Christ.

THE FESTIVAL OF TRUMPETS

for the trumpet shall sound, and the dead shall be raised incorruptible, and we shall be changed . . .
I Corinthians 15: 52

The Lord said to Moses: 'You shall observe a memorial day announced by blowing of trumpets.'
MLB Leviticus 23: 23, 24

If we believe that Jesus died and rose again . . . we shall be caught up to meet the Lord in the air.
I Thessalonians 4: 14-17

Photographs of 'The Crucifixion' and 'The Resurrection' paintings are furnished through the courtesy of Forest Lawn Memorial Park, Glendale, California, where countless visitors see these great works of religious art and are inspired by their dramatic stories.

DAY OF ATONEMENT

The tenth day of the seventh month shall be a day of atonement.
Leviticus 23: 27

And the Lord said to Moses: '*. . . you shall afflict yourselves and present an offering by fire to the Lord.' You shall spend the day in fasting, repentance and sorrow.*
Leviticus 23: 27

The 10 days between the feast of trumpets and the day of atonement were known as 'awesome days' of repentance. For 1900 years, it has not been possible to carry out the day of atonement as God commanded, because there has been no temple. The modern practice is to meet at watering places to perform the symbolic ritual of casting away their sins. A man takes a rooster, a woman a hen. Each one swings it around his or her head saying: 'This is my substitute . . . this rooster (or hen) goes to death; but may I be gathered into a long and happy life and into peace.'

Orthodox Jew — waving rooster

The Mount of Olives

On the day when the Lord Jesus places His feet on the Mount of Olives, the nation of Israel will observe a national day of atonement.

When they look on Him (the Messiah) whom they have pierced they shall mourn for Him as one mourns for his only child.

'On that day,' says the Lord of hosts: 'there shall be a fountain opened . . . to cleanse them from sin and uncleanness.' And the Lord will become King over all the earth.

Zechariah 12: 10, 12; 13: 1; 14: 9

It is the blood that makes atonement for the soul Leviticus 17:11

The Holy of Holies where the High Priest went only on the day of atonement each year

Prior to the destruction of the temple in AD 70, the high priest, on the day of atonement, laid aside his garments of beauty and glory and put on a plain white robe. He then made atonement for himself, and then for the sins of the nation. This was a beautiful picture of the Lord Jesus leaving heaven's glory to put on the robe of His pure humanity in order to make atonement for the sins of the world. As the prophet Isaiah foretold: *He was wounded for our transgressions, He was bruised for our iniquities . . . and the Lord has laid on Him the iniquity of us all.'*

Isaiah 53: 5, 6

THE JOYFUL FESTIVAL OF TABERNACLES
You shall rejoice before the Lord your God seven days   Leviticus 23:40

Take boughs of goodly trees, branches of palm trees, and willows of the brook, . . . you shall dwell in booths seven days to remind you that I rescued you from Egypt.   Leviticus 23: 40, 43

The feast of tabernacles is the seventh of the feasts, observed in the seventh month, and was to last seven days. Seven is the Bible number for completion. It was on the seventh day that God rested from all His work of Creation, Genesis 2: 2. This festival of rejoicing points to the millenium, earth's golden age, when all nations shall beat their weapons of war into implements of peace.

And it shall come to pass that everyone that is left of all the nations which came against Jerusalem shall go up from year to year, to worship the King, the Lord of Hosts, and to keep the feast of tabernacles.   Zechariah 14: 16

During the feast of tabernacles, all meals are eaten in the booth (Succah)

39

SUMMARY OF JEWISH HOLY DAYS
Their prophetic and Christian significance

Date	Jewish Holy Days	Christian Parallel
March — April	Passover	Behold the Lamb of God
March — April	Unleavened Bread	This is my body given for you
March — April	Firstfruits	The Resurrection
May — June	Gathering of Harvest	Pentecost
August — September	Festival of Trumpets	Rapture of the Church
August — September	Day of Atonement	Israel reconciled, redeemed and blessed
August — September	Festival of Tabernacles	The Millenium

GLORIOUS BLESSINGS FOLLOW ISRAEL'S RECOGNITION OF THEIR MESSIAH

For Israel will again be great, filled with joy like that of reapers when the harvest time has come . . . In that glorious day of peace there will no longer be the issuing of battle gear.   TLB Isaiah 9: 3-5

Speak tenderly to Jerusalem, tell her that her sad days are gone, her sins are pardoned, and the Lord will give her twice as many blessings as He gave her punishment before.   TLB Isaiah 40: 2

I will cleanse them from all their iniquity whereby they have sinned against me . . . I will perform that good thing which I have promised to the house of Israel and to the house of Judah.
Jeremiah 33: 8-14

And Jerusalem shall be safe at last, never again to be cursed and destroyed.   Zechariah 14: 11

I'VE BLOTTED OUT YOUR SINS, THEY ARE GONE LIKE MORNING MIST AT NOON! I HAVE PAID THE PRICE TO SET YOU FREE. SING, O HEAVENS, FOR THE LORD HATH DONE THIS WONDROUS THING — FOR THE LORD REDEEMED JACOB AND IS GLORIFIED IN ISRAEL.

ISAIAH 44 2223

The last three festivals of the Jewish calendar are yet to be fulfilled. Leviticus 23 lists all the Jewish festivals in their correct sequence, and is a beautiful picture of God's plan from chaos to earth's golden era. The longest break in Israel's calendar occurs between Pentecost and the festival of trumpets. Similarly, the longest interval during this church age is between Pentecost and the coming day, when *the Lord Himself will descend from heaven with a shout and the great trumpet call of God . . . and we are caught up to meet the Lord in the air, and so shall we be forever with the Lord.*
I Thessalonians 4: 16, 17

You shall not muzzle the ox when he treadeth out the corn

Deuteronomy 25:4

God's directions for the protection of dumb animals should be observed and considered a vital part of our lives. Our first responsibility is love to God and to our fellow men; and secondly, care and proper attention to all of God's creatures.

There were some men and women who, during the second world war, were so cruel to human beings, they sadistically indulged in atrocities which defy description, and at the same time treated their pet animals with tender care.

The title text on this page instructs us to let the ox help itself to food during the monotonous round of corn treading. We are told to leave the birds undisturbed while sitting on their nests. God instructs us not to let an ass be over-burdened by yoking it with an ox. He tells us to rescue any creature fallen into a pit.

A good man is concerned for the welfare of his animals, but even the kindness of a godless man is cruel.

TLB Proverbs 12: 4

God gives the wild animals their food, and the young ravens that cry.

Psalm 149: 9

The God who feeds the wild animals is the God who cares for the body and soul of all who trust Him.

41

The LORD said, '... make Me a sanctuary'

As a visible sign of His presence, God gave Moses detailed instructions regarding the portable tabernacle which later would be erected as a temple by King Solomon on the place of God's choosing in Jerusalem. It was God's desire to dwell in the midst of His people. Today it is His desire to dwell in our hearts. Once God had a temple for His people. Now He has His people for a temple. *Know you not, that your body is the temple of the Holy Spirit . . . you are not your own, you are bought with a price, therefore glorify God in your body.* I Corinthians 6: 19-20

They brought all types of gold objects to be used for the tent of meeting. Every one who could make an offering of silver or bronze or linen or goat's hair . . . onyx stones . . . spices and anointing oil for the fragrant incense . . . all the people of Israel whose heart moved them to bring anything for the work of the Lord. Exodus 35: 19-29

It has been estimated that the gifts brought by the children of Israel were valued at one and a quarter million dollars. These were lavished on them by the Egyptians on the night of their departure. It served as a recompense for their years of slavery. The outer court of the tabernacle was 53.3 metres — 175 feet — long and 26.7 metres —87½ feet — wide. The brazen altar was inside the entrance to the outer court. This teaches us that the only way for sinful man to approach God is on the ground of sacrifice. No person has ever been accepted by God any other way. That is why it was God who first shed the blood of innocent animals to provide a cover for Adam and Eve. Next came the laver for the priests to wash their hands and feet. This speaks of holy conduct and walk. In the holy place, on the right, was the table of shewbread, and on the left, at the south end, was the candlestick. These spoke of Christ as the 'Bread of Life' and as the 'Light of the World.' Just before the veil of the Holy of Holies stood the golden altar of incense symbolising Christ's intercession for us. The Holy of Holies was a perfect cube, 10 by 10 by 10, this spoke of the perfection of God. The ark of the covenant was a gold covered, acacia wood chest. The lid, or mercy seat, had two golden cherubims facing each other. The high priest came once a year to sprinkle the blood of atonement; first on the veil, this spoke of access to God's presence; then before the ark of the covenant, symbolising acceptance by God; and on the mercy seat, fellowship with God. When Jesus Christ said on the cross: *'It is finished',* the veil was rent from the top to the bottom. It was an act of God declaring that the way into His presence was available for redeemed mankind. Because of the beautiful symbolism of the tabernacle, the scriptures devote more time to its description than to any other single subject.

Descending Mount Sinai

They murmured against GOD and craved for the water melons, the cucumbers, the onions, and the garlic they had enjoyed in Egypt

Numbers 11.5

THE LORD SAID: *'BECAUSE OF YOUR UN-FAITHFULNESS YOUR SONS WILL HAVE TO WANDER IN THE WILDERNESS FOR FORTY YEARS.'* YET GOD STILL BLESSED THEM AND THEY LACKED NOTHING. Numbers 14: 33
Deuteronomy 2: 7

Moses went to the top of Mount Nebo east of Jericho, and there the Lord showed him the promised land. *I have let you see it, but I will not let you go there.* So Moses, the Lord's servant, died there. Moses was 120 years old when he died. Israel mourned for him for 30 days in the plains of Moab. · see Deuteronomy 34

He encircled them and tended them with care. He guarded them as the apple of His eye. As an eagle stirs up its nest, hovering over its young . . . so the Lord alone was guide to them.
MLB Deuteronomy 32: 10-12

The Eternal God is thy Refuge, and UNDERNEATH ARE the everlasting Arms.

·DEUTERONOMY· 33·27·

One of the beautiful blessings the Lord gave to Moses to pass on through Aaron and his sons is
The Lord bless you and keep you;
The Lord make His face to shine upon you,
and be gracious unto you;
The Lord lift up His countenance upon
you, and give you peace.
So shall they put My name upon the people
of Israel, and I will bless them. Numbers 6: 24-27

THE PROMISED LAND AT LAST

After forty years of wilderness wanderings.

MOSES' MINISTER BECOMES ISRAEL'S LEADER.

River Jordan

Joshua (son of Nun) was full of the spirit of wisdom, for Moses had laid his hands upon him.

Deuteronomy 34:9

The Lord said unto Joshua the son of Nun: 'Moses my servant is dead, now therefore arise, go over this Jordan, you and all this people, into the land which I am giving to them. Be strong and of good courage; for you shall cause this people to inherit the land which I swore to their fathers to give them.'

Joshua 1: 1-6

In order to cross the flooded Jordan, the people were to follow the priests carrying the ark of the tabernacle (the ark is a symbol of God's presence). *As the feet of the priests touched the water, the waters coming down from the north mounted up in a heap at Adam . . . and those flowing down towards the Dead Sea (Salt Sea), were wholly cut off; and the people passed over opposite Jericho.*

Joshua 3: 15-16

Jericho today

The long desert trek was over, they had reached the promised land at last. A new life in a new country with new conquests ahead, made them curious and cautious. God motivated and inspired the people through their leader, and He said to Joshua five times: *'Be strong and courageous.'* The conquest of Jericho was their first victory. *The Lord said to Joshua: 'I have delivered Jericho . . . into your hand.'* As the Lord instructed, they marched around the walls every day for six days. On the seventh day they marched around seven times, the priests blew their trumpets, the people shouted, and the walls fell down.

Joshua 6

Forty years later Joshua said: *'The Lord gave to Israel all the land which He swore to give to their fathers; and having taken possession of it, they settled there . . . Not one of all the good promises which the Lord had made to the house of Israel had failed; all came to pass.'* Joshua 21: 43-45

46

Obedience, the secret for God's blessing

DIVISION OF THE LAND

Joshua, as an old man, realised there was still much land to be possessed, and at that time he divided the land amongst the tribes, including the land still occupied by other nations, as well as the land already conquered. It was not until the reign of King David that the remainder of the area Joshua had allocated was conquered and occupied. The land of Canaan was approximately 289.6 kilometres — 180 miles — long and 64.3 kilometres — 40 miles — wide. It consisted of the major part of the fertile crescent which lay between Africa and Asia. The Mountains of Lebanon to the north, the Wilderness to the south, the Mediterranian Sea to the west, and the Arabian Desert to the east, defined its boundaries.

'IF YOU FULLY OBEY ALL THE COMMANDMENTS OF THE LORD GOD, BLESSINGS WILL COME UPON YOU.'

Blessings in the City.
Blessings in the Field.
Blessings of Children.
Large Flocks and Herds.
Blessings of Fruit and Bread.
Blessings when you come in.
Blessings when you go out.   Deuteronomy 28: 1-6

Tel Aviv. A modern city in Israel

Every man did that which was right in his own eyes Judges 17:6

Mount Tabor

In those days there was no King in Israel.

Judges 17: 6

The book of Judges covers the first three hundred and fifty years in the land of promise. This period has been described as the dark ages of the children of Israel. The people forsook God and God forsook them. The wilderness wanderers found rehabilitation difficult. Fifteen different judges led the nation during this period.

Professor Moorehead describes the book of Judges as:
Seven apostasies,
Seven servitudes to
Seven heathen nations and
Seven deliverances.

'Deborah, a prophetess, judged Israel . . . she sent and called Barak and said to him: 'The Lord the God of Israel commands you. Go gather your men at Mount Tabor, taking ten thousand men'. . . Barak said to her: 'If you go with me I will go, but if you will not go, I will not go.' Judges 4: 4-8

The Lord accomplished a glorious victory.

A section of the Jezreel Valley

Ruins of Ashkelon. It was once a Philistine city, the place of Samson's exploits

GOD uses an insignificant man for a significant task

Gideon was beating out wheat in the winepress, to hide it from the Midianites, and the angel of the Lord appeared to him and said: 'The Lord is with you, you mighty man of valour. Go in this might of yours and deliver Israel from the hand of the Midian, do not I send you?' Gideon answered: 'Lord, how can I deliver Israel? My clan is the weakest . . . and I am the least in my family.' The Lord said to him: 'I will be with you, and you shall smite the Midianites as one man.'
Judges 6: 11-16

The spring Harod, where Gideon selected his men

When Gideon chose 32 000 men to fight the vast army of the Midianites, the Lord said there were too many, and told Gideon to send home those who were afraid; 10 000 remained and the Lord said: *'There are still too many. Go down to the water and drink.'* Most of the men knelt down to drink, but 300 put their hand to their mouth and lapped the water. The Lord said: *'With these 300 men I will deliver you.'*   Judges 7: 4-7

SAMSON & DELILAH

Samson, a Nazarite from birth, was chosen by God to deliver Israel from the Philistines. They sought the secret of his great strength, and he was betrayed by his wife Delilah. They cut off his hair wherein lay his strength, and took him blinded and bound to Gaza. At a great feast to their god Dagon, the Philistines called in Samson that they might make sport of him. *Samson grasped the two middle pillars . . . and leaned his weight upon them . . . and the house fell upon the lords and upon all the people that were in it. So the ones whom he slew at his death were more than those whom he had slain during his life. He had been a judge in Israel for twenty years.*
Judges 16: 29-31

The spirit of the LORD came upon David I Samuel 16:13

A modern 'David' with his sling

Samuel the prophet was the last of the long line of judges. The people of Israel demanded that he should appoint for them a king. The story of 500 years of royalty began with Saul whose reign ended in disaster. David the shepherd warrior became Israel's second king. *David was ruddy . . . and of a beautiful countenance.*
I Samuel 16: 12

Now the Spirit of the Lord departed from Saul, I Samuel 16: 14.
Saul made five attacks on David's life. David was the anointed, but not the acknowledged king. He was Jesse's son and the great grandson of Ruth and Boaz. He was born in Bethlehem and was the youngest of eight sons. Samuel the prophet had taken the horn of oil to Bethlehem and had anointed him.

When the Israelites were challenged by the giant Goliath, David took his staff in his hand, chose five smooth stones from the brook, and defeated the Philistine with a sling and a stone. David's victory was assured because his faith was in God.

Raisins on drying racks

When Nabal, the very rich farmer, was celebrating with his men at the conclusion of the sheep shearing season, David requested a share in the bounty as his men had protected the shearers. Nabal refused. When David was on his way to retaliate, Nabal's wife Abigail appeased David and took him *two hundred loaves, two skins of wine, five sheep ready dressed, five measures of parched grain, one hundred clusters of raisins and two hundred cakes of figs.* After Nabal's untimely death, David married Abigail. I Samuel 25: 2-42

50

Mount Zion

After reigning in Hebron for seven years David and his men went to Jerusalem and captured the stronghold of Zion and called it the City of David. David became greater and greater for the Lord was with him.   II Samuel 5: 5-10

The nation of Israel became united under his leadership and above everything else he wanted to give God the central place of worship. For this reason he bought the threshing floor of Araunah the Jebusite. This was the place God had chosen, but because David was a man of war it had to be his son Solomon's privilege to build the temple on the site now occupied by the Dome of the Rock. Nathan the prophet said to David: '. . . *your house and your kingdom shall be made sure for ever.'*   II Samuel 7: 8-16
The Messiah, Jesus Christ, as descendant of King David is the fulfilment of this covenant.

David's rebel son, Absalom, had no sons to carry on his name. He erected a memorial to himself in the Kidron Valley. The present memorial, dating back to the first century A.D., is commonly called Absalom's Pillar. Many people throw stones at the memorial in contempt of the man who dishonoured his father.

David the sweet Psalmist of Israel,

Praise Him with stringed instruments

The Psalms are often referred to as the hymns of Israel. They consist of a delightful combination of worship, praise, personal experiences, prophecies, Messianic predictions, benedictions, challenges, repentance, and comfort. God's blessing in the past, His daily provision for the present, and glorious prospects for the future, are recorded in this book. Psalms 120 to 134 are usually acknowledged as the Songs of Degrees which the Children of Israel sang on their ascent to Jerusalem for the three annual feasts of Passover, Pentecost, and Tabernacles. David, who wrote approximately half of the Psalms, constantly expressed his delight in the word of God and in the will of God. Jesus explained to the disciples how the Psalms predicted His coming, first as the Suffering Saviour, then as the Coming King.   Luke 24: 44

The LORD is my shepherd

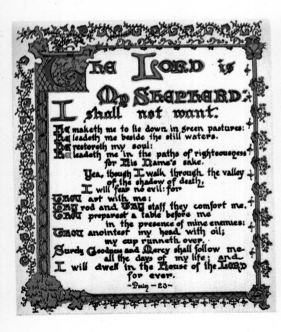

a man after GOD'S own heart

I am like a lonely bird on a housetop. Psalm 102: 7

He sends the snow in all its lovely whiteness.
TLB Psalm 147: 16

'Come now and let us reason together,' says the Lord: "though your sins are like scarlet, they shall be as white as snow.' Isaiah 1: 18

I praise Thee, because I have been fearfully and wonderfully made Psalm 139:14

The Lord touches the mountains and they smoke.
Psalm 104: 32

Even the sparrow finds a home, and the swallow a nest for herself, where she may lay her young.
Psalm 84: 3

Great is the Lord and greatly to be praised, and his greatness is unsearchable. One generation shall praise thy works to another, and shall declare thy mighty acts. My mouth shall speak the praise of the Lord. Let all flesh bless His holy name for ever.
Psalm 145: 3, 4, 21

I have been young; now I am old, yet I have not seen the righteous forsaken or his children begging bread.
Psalm 37: 25

Old age for the believer is not a matter of going downhill, but up and up until the gates of glory come into view.

A cobbler at Beersheba

The cattle on a thousand hills are mine.

Psalm 50: 10

The Lord did not offer one of His own creatures as an animal sacrifice. They have no will of their own. The Lord Jesus offered Himself voluntarily as a ransom for us.

Thou dost show me the path of life; in Thy presence is fulness of joy, at Thy right hand are pleasures for evermore. Psalm 16: 11

King Solomon was richer and wiser than any other king

2 Chronicles 9:22

Modern Eilat stands on the site of Eziongeber, Solomon's port

It pleased the Lord that Solomon had asked for wisdom, and God said: *'Because you have asked this, and not asked for long life or riches . . . I will give you a wise and discerning mind so that none like you has been before and none like you shall arise after; I will give also what you have not asked, both riches and honour.'*

I Kings 3: 10-13

Solomon wrote 3000 proverbs and 1005 songs. On hearing reports of Solomon's wisdom and wealth, the Queen of Sheba visited him in Jerusalem and said: *'. . . behold the half was not told me; your wisdom and prosperity surpass the report which I heard. Happy are these your servants, who continually stand before you and hear your wisdom. Blessed be the Lord your God, who has delighted in you and set you on the throne of Israel. Because the Lord loved Israel for ever, he has made you king, that you may execute justice and righteousness.'* I Kings 10: 6-9

King Solomon's Pillars

The beach front of Tyre

The Dome of the Rock which now occupies the Temple site

Excavated section of Megiddo

In the days of Solomon, King Hiram of Tyre provided him with materials and craftsmen for the building of the temple. Today Tyre is a fishing village.

Megiddo was one of the cities which Solomon walled and fortified. Twenty levels of civilisations have been excavated here. The Megiddo, or Jezreel, Valley has been classified as a battlefield. It is the prophesied location of Armageddon.

Solomon's reign was one of peace and prosperity. His greatest accomplishment was the building of a magnificent temple. It took seven years to build, requiring a workforce of 70 000 labourers. At its dedication, Solomon blessed the people, and said: *'Blessed be the Lord, the God of Israel, who has fulfilled what He promised to my father, David ... Behold the heavens cannot contain Thee, much less this house ... yet Thou hast said, My name shall be there.'*

I Kings 8: 22-29

Solomon rose to great heights, but fell to disappointing depths because he forsook the God of his fathers when he married foreign women. He followed their strange gods and idolatrous practices.

The high hills are a refuge for the wild goats . . . the sun knoweth his going down.
                                                      Psalm 104: 18, 19

As the hart panteth after the waterbrooks, so panteth my soul after thee, O God.
                                                      Psalm 42: 1

My soul thirsteth for God, for the living God: Why art thou cast down, O my soul, and why art thou disquieted within me? Hope thou in God: for I shall yet praise Him, who is the health of my countenance, and my God.
                                                      Psalm 42: 2, 11

David compares his longing heart to the panting hart. The urgent need of his soul was to have the enjoyment of communion with his God, a need far greater than for anything else, whether it be honour, or pleasure, or popularity.

United we stand, divided we fall

After Solomon's great reign, the nation was divided into two separate kingdoms. Israel to the north, Judah to the south. This ushered in the time of the prophets who, during the dark days of Israel and Judah, were likened to watchmen who looked beyond the horizon to the future. Their inspired writings gave instructions, followed by warnings of judgment if the instructions were not obeyed. Many of the prophets also wrote of a Messiah who would suffer and die for man's sin, as told in the verse below, (see complete chapter of Isaiah 53), and of His ultimate righteous reign as King over all kings. This will usher in universal peace and blessing.

All we like sheep have gone astray: We have turned every one to his own way; and the Lord hath laid on Him the iniquity of us all.   Isaiah 53: 6

Watchtower, as seen in Middle East countries

They that wait upon the Lord shall renew their strength; they shall mount up with wings as eagles; they shall run and not be weary; they shall walk and not faint.   Isaiah 40: 31

Fire from heaven. Elijah's God triumphs

Overlooking the city of Haifa from Mount Carmel

Elijah the prophet, and Ahab the king, exerted strong influences over the nation; one for good, the other for evil. The king forsook the commandments of the Lord and encouraged the worship of Baal with its accompanying sinful practices. Elijah was a mighty witness for God. He called all Israel to assemble on Mount Carmel, and said: *'HOW LONG ARE YOU GOING TO WAVER BETWEEN TWO OPINIONS? IF THE LORD IS GOD, FOLLOW HIM, BUT IF BAAL IS GOD, THEN FOLLOW HIM.'*   TLB I Kings 18: 21

Elijah stood alone, taunting the 450 prophets of Baal to call on their god to send down fire to consume their sacrifice, but their religious rituals were ineffective. At sunset, Elijah repaired the broken altar of the Lord. He then drenched the altar and the sacrifice with water, and as Elijah prayed, *the fire of the Lord consumed the sacrifice, and all the people fell on their faces and said: 'The Lord, He is God; the Lord, He is God.'* The full story is told in I Kings 18: 20-40.

Wadi-Kelt as it appears today. Ever since the days of Elijah and Elisha, men have gone to Wadi-Kelt for meditation and seclusion.

Elisha watches Elijah's spectacular departure

Fifty of the young prophets watched from a distance . . . Elijah struck the water with his cloak . . . the river Jordan divided and they went across on dry ground . . . and suddenly Elijah was carried by a whirlwind into heaven. Full story: II Kings 2.

Naaman the Syrian Commander in Chief was a leper. He arrived in Israel with his horses and chariots and stood at the door of Elisha's home. Elisha sent a messenger to the door telling him to wash in the Jordan river seven times and all trace of leprosy would be gone. Naaman was angry and said: *'Aren't the Abana River and the Pharpar River at Damascus far better than all the rivers of Israel?'* An officer persuaded him to try washing in the Jordan, *and his flesh became as a little child's.* Full story: II Kings: 5.

River Jordan

An Arab market in Israel

When the Syrians surrounded Samaria, the famine became so severe in the city that even a donkey's head cost a small fortune. Elisha prophesied that flour and barley would be sold quite cheaply the next day, at the gate of Samaria. The fascinating story is told in II Kings 6 and 7.

The prophet who went west, when God told him to go east

Port of Jaffa (Joppa)

An artist's impression of Nineveh

Jonah rose to flee . . . from the presence of the Lord. He went down to Joppa and found a ship going to Tarshish; so he paid the fare, and went on board.
Jonah 1:3

Nineveh was the capital of Assyria. It was situated on the east bank of the Tigris River. The city was as great in wickedness as it was in wealth and power.

Arise go to Nineveh, that great city, and preach against them.
Jonah 1: 2

The book of Jonah tells of two amazing miracles. Jonah's preservation in the great fish God prepared, and the repentance of the inhabitants of Nineveh by the preaching of an obscure foreign missionary.

An artist's impression of Nineveh. Photograph taken from the 'Wonders of the Past.'

And the people of Nineveh proclaimed a fast, and put on sackcloth from the greatest to the least. They repented at Jonah's preaching, and God abandoned His plan to destroy them. *This change of plans made Jonah very angry. He complained to the Lord about it: 'This is exactly what I thought you would do, Lord, when I was there in my own country, and you first told me to come here. That is why I ran away to Tarshish, for I knew you were a gracious God, merciful and slow to get angry, and full of kindness. I knew how easily you could cancel your plans for destroying these people.'*

Jonah 3, 4

Approximately one hundred and fifty years later Nineveh was destroyed. God's mercy always precedes His judgment. They defied God; they illtreated their enemies. They signed their own death warrant. The Tigris River freak flooded and undermined the so called impregnable walls of the city, allowing the enemy to overthrow them.

Israeli stamps depicting the story of Jonah

After being the mistress of the East for over 400 years Nineveh vanished. God said He would dig her grave, and all trace of Nineveh disappeared for 2 600 years. *'Flocks would lie in the midst of her'* said the prophet. Today they graze on the site of the once flourishing city.

Israel shall serve the King of Babylon for seventy years

You have not listened although the Lord persistently sent to you his prophets, saying: 'Turn now, every one of you, from his evil way . . . do not go after other gods . . . or provoke me to anger . . . so that you can remain in the land which the Lord has given you . . . Therefore, thus saith the Lord of Hosts, Because you have not obeyed my words . . . I will send for Nebuchadnezzar the king of Babylon . . . and I will bring him against this land and the whole land shall become a ruin and a waste . . . and you shall serve the king of Babylon seventy years.' Jeremiah 25: 1-11

Jeremiah the prophet had no way of knowing Judah's captivity would last seventy years apart from Divine inspiration. Why seventy years? Israel was commanded to rest their land one year in every seven. They failed to observe this law for four hundred and ninety years. *Then the land shall enjoy her sabbaths as long as it lies desolate, while you are in your enemies' land.*

Leviticus 26: 34
II Chronicles 36: 21

By the waters of Babylon, there we sat down . . . we wept when we remembered Zion. We hanged our harps upon the willows. Psalm 137: 1, 2

River at Babylon

Ishtar Gate now housed in the Pergamon Museum, East Berlin. This was the most famous of the eight gates leading into the city of Babylon.

64

The 'rise and fall' of four major world powers

King Nebuchadnezzar of Babylon dreamt what he felt was a very significant dream, but he was not able to recall it. He threatened to kill all his wise men if they failed to describe and interpret his dream. Amongst his advisers was Daniel, who requested more time so that he, with his friends, who were captives from Israel, could seek the answer from the God of heaven. Daniel praised God when it was revealed to him and said: *'Blessed be the name of God for ever and ever, to whom belong wisdom and might . . . He removes kings and sets up kings.*

Daniel 2: 1-24

Daniel answered the king: 'No wise men . . . can show the mystery of the dream . . . but there is a God in heaven who reveals mysteries, and He has made known to the king what shall come to pass . . . You saw, O king . . . a great image . . . The head of this image was of fine gold, its breast and arms of silver, its belly and thighs of bronze, its legs of iron, its feet partly of iron and partly of clay.'

Daniel 2: 21-33

The image was made of four metals decreasing in value from gold to iron:
GOLD: representing Babylon the first world empire;
SILVER: the second world empire of Medo-Persia;
BRONZE: the third world empire of Greece;
IRON: the fourth world empire of Rome.

Daniel 2: 36-40

Note the structure is top heavy; gold is heavier than silver, silver than bronze, bronze than iron. Each empire degenerated and distintegrated.

The Lord has stirred up the spirit of the kings of the Medes to march on Babylon and destroy her. This is His vengeance on those who wronged His people and desecrated His temple.

TLB Jeremiah 51: 11

Archaeological wonders dating back to Old Testament times abound in the area of Babylon and Iraq

O Daniel, greatly beloved of God, be strong and of good courage

Daniel 10:19

BABYLON, THE GLORY OF KINGDOMS . . . SHALL BECOME LIKE SODOM AND GOMORRAH, WHEN GOD OVERTHREW THEM. IT WILL NEVER BE INHABITED OR DWELT IN FOR ALL GENERATIONS, NO ARAB WILL PITCH HIS TENT THERE, NO SHEPHERDS WILL MAKE THEIR FLOCKS LIE DOWN THERE. Isaiah 13: 19-20

A PROPHECY LITERALLY FULFILLED SOME CENTURIES LATER.

During the captivity in Babylon Daniel was one of the young men who kept clean in body and soul.

Left: Intricate brickwork as on the Ishtar Gate foundations depicts bulls and dragons representing the gods Hadad and Marduk.

Extreme left: The procession street called in Babylonian AI-IBUR-SHABU — meaning the enemy will never pass.

They thought their city was impregnable.

Jackals will dwell in the pleasant palaces.
Isaiah 13: 22

Extreme left: The archaeologists have found this tablet which verifies the date (597 B.C.) when Jehoiachin, the king reigning in Jerusalem, surrendered to Nebuchadnezzar, king of Babylon.

The LORD gave the remnant of His people a desire to rebuild the temple   Haggai 1:14

View of the Temple Model. Holy Land Hotel

RETURN FROM EXILE

The three post exile prophets were: HAGGAI, ZECHARIAH, and MALACHI.

Prior to the exile, the prophets gave a message of warning,
During the exile a message of hope,
After the exile a message of encouragement.

God says to the returned exiles: *'Is it time for you yourselves to dwell in paneled houses, while the House of the Lord lies in ruins?'*
MLB Haggai 1: 4

The temple had to be rebuilt before the Messiah came as Malachi prophesied: *'The Lord whom you seek will suddenly come to His Temple.'*
Malachi 3: 1

A wonderful message of promise was given them three months after they commenced building the temple.
'The desire of the nations shall come, and I will fill this house with glory. The glory of this latter house will be greater than the former . . . and I will give peace,' says the Lord of Hosts. In this rebuilt temple men saw the glory of God in the face of Jesus Christ. Just imagine what it will be like when He reigns in Jerusalem in dazzling splendour and glory.
Haggai 2: 7, 9

I stole out at night on my donkey to inspect the broken down walls of Jerusalem.   Nehemiah 2: 13
The city of Jerusalem to which Nehemiah returned, was quite small in comparison with modern Jerusalem.

I am against you O Tyre, and I will bring many nations against you   Ezekiel 26:3

Six prophecies were made concerning Tyre.
1. Nebuchadnezzar would attempt to destroy it.
2. Other nations would come against it.
3. Its buildings would be laid into the sea.
4. It would be made flat like the top of a flat rock.
5. It would become a fishing village.
6. Never again to become the major city that it was, whose 'merchant navy' went as far as Britain. They were the world's greatest sailors.

When Alexander the Great invaded Tyre he destroyed the area on the main land and built a causeway with the rubble. This gave him access to the island city. The prophecies of Ezekiel 26:3-5 were fulfilled in detail.

Pella, capital of ancient Macedonia (Greece)
Birthplace of Alexander the Great and his seat of government

Fishermen's nets now hang where Alexander the Great built the causeway

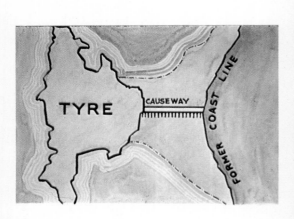

Between the Old and New Testaments (approximately 400 years)

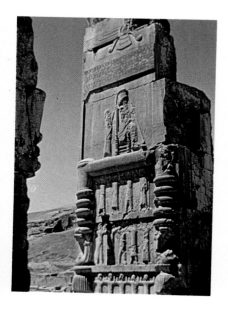

THE PERSIAN PERIOD — 430-332 B.C.

In the main, the Persian rule was very tolerant, except when the King's 'Prime Minister', Haman, received permission to annihilate every Jew. Had that happened, the Messiah would never have been born. The wonderful deliverance is told in the Book of Esther which is read in all synagogues during the festival of Purim. Every time wicked Haman's name is read these clackers are used to denounce him. Ahasuerus, who married Esther, is standing behind his father Darius.

THE GREEK PERIOD — 331-167 B.C.

Alexander the Great at the age of 20, in 336 B.C., became commander of the Greek army. Within a few years, he accomplished his ambition to conquer what he considered to be the world. He spared Jerusalem and showed kindness to the Jews. He established Greek cities, Greek cultures and the Greek language.
This pan-Greek culture, or Hellenism, became a very real threat to the Jews and their faith. For example, the Maccabean Revolt initially was against Hellenism, the great watershed of secular history.

PERIOD OF INDEPENDENCE (THE MACCABEAN PERIOD) — 167-63 B.C.

ROMAN PERIOD — 63 B.C. to time of Christ.

ALL ROADS LED TO ROME. The Roman authorities little realised that their highways, and the elimination of frontiers, and the common trade language, would combine to speed the spread of the 'Good News.'

Centre: A partly reconstructed theatre, Athens

Left: A section of the Roman Forum

They shall suck the abundance of the seas   Deuteronomy 33:19

The Dead Sea is 394 metres — 1292 feet — below sea level, the lowest place on earth. It is 78.3 kilometres — 47 miles — long and 18.3 kilometres — 11 miles — wide. It is called:

The Sea of the Plain	Deuteronomy 4: 49
The Salt Sea	Deuteronomy 3: 17
The East Sea	Joel 2: 20
The former sea	Zechariah 14: 8

For a prophecy yet to be fulfilled concerning the Dead Sea refer Ezekiel 47: 8-10.

The verse quoted at the top of the page was written approximately 3500 years ago. It is being fulfilled today in the extracting of chemicals from the Dead Sea. These chemicals are worth millions of dollars.

Evidence of its amazing buoyancy

A sample of the freak formations

THE DEAD SEA SCROLLS and their significance

Included in the discovery were portions of all the Old Testament books with the exception of the book of Esther. The scroll of Isaiah is 7.3 metres — 24 feet — long and is the central feature in the building in Jerusalem known as the 'Shrine of the Book'. The building is shaped to resemble the lid of the jars in which the scrolls were found. They greatly contribute to our knowledge of Judaism and Christianity and demonstrate the high degree of accuracy maintained in hand copying and printing during the past 2000 years. Written between 150 B.C. and 68 A.D. they show a variety of literature such as a collection of hymns, prayers, Bible commentaries, disciplinary manuals and Messianic prophecies. The scrolls belonged to the Essenes, a monastic Jewish brotherhood who practised strong disciplines and lived for the coming of two Messiahs, a priestly Messiah, and a military Messiah. There is evidence that some fled to Massada during the Roman purge.

The QUMRAN CAVES where the Bedouin boy found the jars containing what we now know as the Dead Sea Scrolls. This cave (No 4) contained 10000 fragments, which must be the world's largest jigsaw puzzle.

Interior of the Shrine of the Book showing the scroll of Isaiah

Shrine of the Book

Rejoice with Jerusalem, be glad with her,

Jerusalem

Jerusalem, the city where I have chosen to place my name.
I Kings 11: 36

Rejoice with Jerusalem, be glad with her, all you who love her.
Isaiah 66: 10

Pray for the peace of Jerusalem; they shall prosper that love thee.
Psalm 122: 6

The Bible predicts that when they acknowledge Him whom they pierced, *Jerusalem shall be . . . safe at last, never again to be cursed and destroyed.*
TLB Zechariah 14: 11

The Nerve centre of the world, geographically   Ezekiel 5:5
The Salvation centre of the world, spiritually   John 4: 22
The Trouble centre of the world, prophetically Zechariah 14: 1-8
The Glory centre of the world, ultimately   Isaiah 2: 1-5

all you who love her Isaiah 66:10

Chronology of Jerusalem

2000	B.C.	Melchizedek, King of Salem (Jerusalem) brought Abraham bread and wine Abraham offered Isaac on Mt Moriah
1000	B.C.	David captured the city
961-922	B.C.	Solomon beautified the city and built the temple
800	B.C.	Uzziah
700	B.C.	Hezekiah
641-610	B.C.	Josiah
587	B.C.	City destroyed by Nebuchadnezzar of Babylon
539	B.C.	Persian occupation
520-516	B.C.	Zerubbabel's Temple
446	B.C.	Nehemiah rebuilds the walls
165	B.C.	Maccabeans
63	B.C.	The Romans captured the city
37	B.C.	Herod appointed King. He rebuilds the temple
41	A.D.	Herod Agrippa
70	A.D.	Destruction under Titus. Titus ploughed up a portion of Jerusalem
131	A.D.	Hadrian rebuilt the city and named it Aelia Capitolina
330-337	A.D.	Constantine the Great first 'Christian' emperor restored the name of Jerusalem
636	A.D.	Jerusalem passed to the Arabs who held it for almost 500 years
641	A.D.	The Persians conquered Jerusalem and destroyed all its churches
969	A.D.	Selzuk Turks
1099	A.D.	Crusaders
1187	A.D.	Saladin
1517-1917	A.D.	Ottoman Empire
1917	A.D.	Taken by the Allies under General Allenby, Balfour Declaration
1948	A.D.	State of Israel declared: *'There has always been and always will be one capital only, Jerusalem the eternal. Thus it was 3000 years ago and thus it will be, we believe, until the end of time.'* David Ben Gurion
1967	A.D.	Six Day War. Jerusalem occupied by the Israelis

The LORD your GOD shall choose a place to put His name,

Mount Moriah

The temple area became a Moslem shrine in 1187 A.D.

Four thousand years of history interspersed with Sacrifices, Songs, Shekinah Glory, Magnificent Temples, Travail and Triumph, make this site the most sacred shrine to the sons of Israel. It is the third most sacred site to the Moslems, and treasured memories stir the Christians as they contemplate the ministry of the Son of God, and the prophecies and promises He made concerning this site.

Dome made of aluminium bronze alloy

Below is a summary of major events:

David purchases the threshing floor from Araunah the Jebusite.   II Samuel 24: 24

David purchases the whole hill from Araunah.   I Chronicles 21: 25

Solomon built his temple here.   II Chronicles 3: 1

Completed after seven years in 950 B.C. Destroyed by Nebuchadnezzar in 587 B.C.

Zerubbabel rebuilt the temple in 520 B.C.   Ezra 5: 2; 6: 15

Herod the Great built a temple. Begun in 20 B.C. and finished 64 A.D.

Jesus was presented in the temple.   Luke 2: 22

Jesus returned at twelve years of age.   Luke 2: 41

Our Lord drives out the money changers.   John 2: 13

Jesus attends the Feast of Tabernacles.   John 7: 10

Woman taken in adultery.   John 8: 1-11

Jesus said: *'I am the Light of the World.'*   John 8: 12-32

　　　　　'I am the Good Shepherd.'   John 10: 1-18

Jesus' judgment on Pharisees and Sadducees.   Matthew 21: 23

Peter and John go to the temple to pray.   Acts 3: 1

Paul returns to Jerusalem.   Acts 21: 15

Temple was destroyed by Titus in 70 A.D.

Emperor Hadrian marched into Jerusalem and Moriah became paganised by Roman Jupiter worshippers in 135 A.D.

Emperor Justinian built foundations for the new Church of St Mary in 534 A.D.

Moriah became a Moslem shrine in 639 A.D. Mohammed is said to have made his leap to heaven from here.

Crusaders erect the Templum Domini in 1099 A.D.

Became a Moslem shrine in 1187 A.D. which remains to this day.

there you shall offer your burnt offerings Deuteronomy 12:11

Jews from all over the world return to the western wall to pray. This outer wall of the temple's perimeter, featured right, is all that is left of Herod's temple. This area is used for worship and national celebrations. The following verse is an appropriate prayer.

'O Lord, cause thy face to shine upon thy sanctuary which is desolate.' Daniel 9: 17

For thy servants hold her stones dear . . . The Lord will build up Zion, He will appear in His glory. Psalm 102: 14-16

Inside the dome is the rock, reputed to be where Abraham was prepared to offer Isaac as a sacrifice

His name shall be called Wonderful, Counsellor, the Mighty God,

A SELECTION OF OLD TESTAMENT MESSIANIC PROPHECIES

Jacob predicted the tribe from which the Messiah would come.
David foretold the family.
Daniel prophesied the date.
Isaiah described the channel (a virgin).
Micah predicted the place.
Moses wrote of the coming Messiah as being the *seed of the woman.* Seed is always masculine, this exception points to the day when *a virgin shall conceive and bear a son, and they shall call His name IMMANUEL.*   Isaiah 7: 14

MESSIAH WAS TO ENTER JERUSALEM IN TRIUMPH

Rejoice greatly, O daughter of Zion; shout, O daughter of Jerusalem; behold thy King cometh unto thee: He is just, and having salvation: lowly, and riding upon an ass and upon a colt the foal of an ass.   Zechariah 9: 9
Refer Matthew 21: 1-9; John 12: 12-16

MESSIAH WAS TO BE REJECTED BY HIS OWN PEOPLE

Who hath believed our report? And to whom is the arm of the Lord revealed? He is despised and rejected of men; a man of sorrows and acquainted with grief; and we hid as it were our faces from Him; He was despised, and we esteemed Him not.
                Isaiah 53: 1-2

See John 1: 11-12; John 12: 37-43

MESSIAH WAS TO BE BETRAYED BY ONE OF HIS FOLLOWERS

Yea, mine own familiar friend, in whom I trusted, which did eat of my bread, hath lifted up his heel against me. Psalm 41: 9
New Testament fulfilment: see Matthew 26: 14-16, 47-50; Mark 14: 17-21

MESSIAH WAS TO BE TRIED AND CONDEMNED

He was taken from prison and from judgment: and who shall declare His generation? For He was cut off out of the land of the living: for the transgression of my people was He stricken.
                Isaiah 53: 8; Matthew 27: 1-2; Luke 23: 1-25

MESSIAH WAS TO BE SILENT BEFORE HIS ACCUSERS

He was oppressed, and He was afflicted, yet He opened not His mouth: He is brought as a lamb to the slaughter, and as a sheep before her shearers is dumb, so He opened not His mouth.
                Isaiah 53: 7; Matthew 27: 12-14; Mark 15: 3-4; Luke 23: 8-10

Over the entrance porch of the Young Men's Christian Association, Jerusalem. This outstanding prophecy is from Isaiah 9: 6, attesting to the deity and the humanity of the Messiah.

Herod's Palace (model at Holy Land Hotel) to which the wise men came seeking the *One born King of the Jews.* Herod killed all the boys in Bethlehem two years old and under but the 'King' was being sheltered in Egypt. Jeremiah's prophecy describes the resultant sorrow of *Rachel weeping for her children.*
                Jeremiah 31: 15

the Everlasting Father, the Prince of Peace Isaiah 9:6

MESSIAH WAS TO BE SMITTEN AND SPAT UPON

They shall smite the judge of Israel with a rod upon the cheek.
Micah 5: 1

I gave my back to the smiters, and my cheeks to them that plucked off the hair. I hid not my face from shame and spitting.
Isaiah 50: 6

See Matthew 26: 67; Matthew 27: 30; Mark 14: 65

MESSIAH WAS TO BE MOCKED AND TAUNTED

All they that see me laugh me to scorn: they shoot out the lip, they shake the head, saying, He trusted on the LORD that He would deliver Him; let Him deliver Him, seeing He delighted in Him.
Psalm 22: 7-8
New Testament fulfilment: see Matthew 27: 39-43; Luke 23: 11, 35.

MESSIAH WAS TO DIE BY CRUCIFIXION

They pierced my hands and my feet. I may tell all my bones: they look and stare upon me.
Psalm 22: 14, 16-17
See Matthew 27: 31; Mark 15: 20; John 19: 15-18.

MESSIAH WAS TO SUFFER WITH CRIMINALS AND PRAY FOR HIS ENEMIES

And He was numbered with the transgressors; and He bare the sin of many, and made intercession for the transgressors.
Isaiah 53: 12

See Matthew 27: 38; Mark 15: 27-28; Luke 23: 32-34

MESSIAH WAS TO BE GIVEN VINEGAR AND GALL

They gave me also gall for my meat; and in my thirst they gave me vinegar to drink.
Psalm 69: 21
New Testament fulfilment: see Matthew 27: 34; John 19: 28-30.

THEY WERE TO CAST LOTS FOR MESSIAH'S GARMENTS

They parted my garments among them, and cast lots upon my vesture.
Psalm 22: 18
See Matthew 27: 35; Mark 15: 24; John 19: 23-24.

MESSIAH'S BONES NOT TO BE BROKEN

Not a bone of His shall be broken.   Refer Psalm 34: 20
New Testament fulfilment: see John 19: 31-36.
Because the next day was a holy day the Jews asked Pilate that their legs might be broken, and that they might be taken away. So the soldiers came and broke the legs of the first, and of the other who had been crucified with Him; but when they came to Jesus and saw that He was already dead, they did not break His legs.

MESSIAH WAS TO DIE AS A SACRIFICE FOR SIN

But He was wounded for our transgressions. He was bruised for our iniquities; the chastisement of our peace was upon Him; and with His stripes we are healed. All we like sheep have gone astray; we have turned every one to His own way; and the Lord hath laid on Him the iniquity of us all . . . For the transgression of my people was He stricken . . . When thou shalt make His soul an offering for sin, He shall see His seed, He shall prolong His days, and the pleasure of the Lord shall prosper in His hand . . . He shall bear their iniquities . . . and He bare the sin of many.
Isaiah 53: 5, 6, 8, 10-12
See John 1: 29; John 11: 49-52; Acts 10-43; John 1: 7, 9.

MESSIAH WAS TO BE RAISED FROM THE DEAD

For thou wilt not leave my soul in hell; neither wilt thou suffer thine Holy One to see corruption.   Psalm 16: 10
See Acts 2: 22-32; Matthew 28: 1-10

MESSIAH NOW AT GOD'S RIGHT HAND

The Lord said to my Lord, 'Sit thou at my right hand, until I make thine enemies thy footstool.'   Psalm 110: 1

NOTE: The above are only some of the many Old Testament prophecies of Messiah that were fulfilled in Jesus Christ.

One of the Dead Sea Scrolls consisted of a collection of writings from the Old Testament highlighting Messianic Prophecies including the verse: *'The sceptre shall not depart from Judah, nor the ruler's staff from between his feet until Shiloh come; and unto Him shall the gathering of the people be'.*
Genesis 49: 10
During the major transition period — B.C. to A.D. — the sceptre departed from Israel.

Bible history and types as well as the Psalms and the Prophets converge toward one supreme event — the coming of the Messiah. His atoning sacrifice and His ultimate reign in righteousness will usher in universal peace.

In the plan and purposes of God we see that the Old Testament writers pointed forward to Jesus Christ in so many ways. This is just one of the indications we have that the mind of Deity supervised the writing and shaping of the Bible.

THE NEW TESTAMENT

JOY TO THE WORLD

THE FATHER

My Son,
Farewell.
A body I've prepared
for you
in Mary
Jewish girl
betrothed to Joseph
Jewish carpenter.
You who have been with me
from everlasting days
who with me made all things
including earth and man
and Mary
tonight become
a creature vulnerable
baby most helpless.
The swirling cloud
takes you to her
through darkest night.
I send an angel army
to protect
proclaim your birth.

You'll grow
and spend a few days' light
then darkest noon
and you'll return.
I'll have the dust of earth
the virgin's fruit
at my right hand
forevermore.
Tonight I joy
that you delight to do my will
take God-sized step
to earth and womb
and tree.
My Son, Farewell
I hear a baby's cry.

Christmas Voices Joseph Bayly, 1974

From *Decision*   by the Billy Graham
Evangelistic Association

JESUS THE MESSIAH

He comes,
The Light of the World,
The Bread of Life,
The Prince of Peace,
The Lamb of God,
The Reconciler of Man to God,
The Central Figure of History,
The Perfect Man who obeyed a
  Perfect law, qualifying Him
  to become a Perfect Saviour.
Great is the Mystery of Godliness,
God was made visible in human flesh.
He came from the bosom of the
  Father to the arms of a
  Jewish mother.

78

HAIL! You are highly favoured. Blessed are you among women
Luke 1:28

God sent the angel Gabriel to Nazareth . . . to a virgin named Mary, engaged to be married to Joseph, a descendant of King David. Luke 1: 26-27

Gabriel: *Fear not, Mary . . . behold you will bring forth a Son and you shall call His name Jesus.*
Luke 1: 30-31

Mary: *How can this be, since I am a virgin?*
Luke 1: 34

Gabriel: *The Holy Spirit will come upon you . . . therefore the child to be born will be called holy, the Son of God.* Luke 1: 35

Gabriel: *Fear not Joseph . . . to take to you Mary as your wife, for that which is conceived in her is from the Holy Spirit. And she shall bring forth a Son, and you shall call His name Jesus, for He shall save His people from their sins.*
Matthew 1: 20-21

Nazareth

Elizabeth· *Blessed be the fruit of your womb . . . and how have I deserved this honour that the mother of my Lord should come to me?* Luke 1: 42-43

Mary's answer, usually spoken of as the Magnificat, is featured in forty-two languages on plaques such as this.

The Church on the traditional site of Mary's meeting with Elizabeth Refer: Luke 1: 39-40

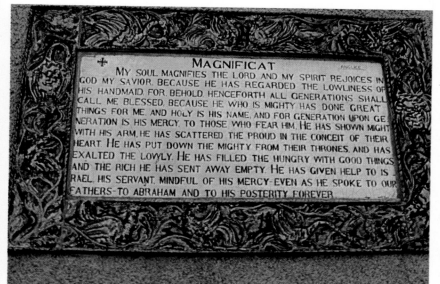

And everyone went to be registered, each to his own city Luke 2:3

So Joseph went from Nazareth . . . to the City of Bethlehem . . . to be registered with Mary his betrothed wife . . . and she brought forth her first-born son, and she wrapped Him in swaddling clothes and laid Him in a manger, because there was no room in the inn. Luke 2: 4-7

The prophecy of Micah, written approximately 700 years before, was fulfilled at Christ's birth. It reads, *O Bethlehem Ephratah, you are but a small Judean village, yet you will be the birthplace of my King who is alive from everlasting ages past.* MLB Micah 5: 2

Bethlehem, where Jesus was born

The Silver Star in the grotto of the Church of the Nativity bears the Latin inscription 'Here Jesus was born of the Virgin Mary'

Looking down from the Church of the Nativity to the grotto, the traditional birth-place of Jesus

Tidings of great joy

'The bells on the Church of the Nativity can be heard over the radio in many countries on Christmas Day

In that region there were shepherds out in the field, keeping watch over their flock by night. And an angel of the Lord appeared to them, and the glory of the Lord shone round about them. And the angel said to them: 'Behold I bring you tidings of great joy that will come to all people; for to you is born this day in the city of David a Saviour, who is Christ the Lord.' Luke 2: 8-11

The wise men came from the East to worship the new born King

Rise . . . flee to Egypt

An angel of the Lord appeared to Joseph in a dream, and said: 'Rise, and flee to Egypt, and remain there till I tell you: for Herod is about to search for the child to destroy him' . . . This was to fulfil what the Lord had spoken by the prophet, 'Out of Egypt have I called my son.'

Hosea 2: 1
Matthew 2: 13-15

Bas-relief in grotto at Bethlehem, depicting the flight to Egypt

A carpenter's bench serves as the communion table in the chapel of the Edinburgh Medical Missionary Hospital at Nazareth

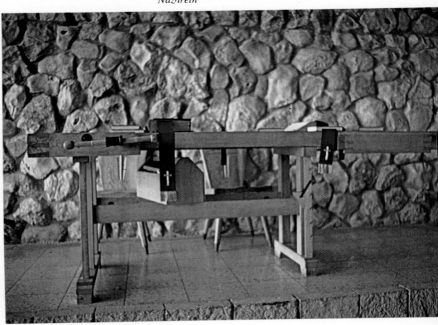

When Herod died, Joseph took the child and His mother and went to the land of Israel . . . and He came and dwelt in a city called Nazareth: that it might be fulfilled which was spoken by the prophets, He shall be called a Nazarene. Matthew 2: 23

At twelve years of age Jesus accompanied His family to Jerusalem for the Passover. He was missing for three days and was found by his parents teaching in the temple. He returned with them to Nazareth and lived under their authority, and *Jesus grew in wisdom, stature, and favour with God and man.* Luke 2: 52

Jesus is the working man's friend. He spent more time working in Nazareth, probably at the carpenter's bench, than in His earth-shaking ministry.

JOHN HERALDS CHRIST'S ARRIVAL

In those days John the Baptist came, preaching in the wilderness of Judea, 'Repent, for the kingdom of heaven is at hand.' For this is he who was spoken of by the prophet Isaiah when he said, 'The voice of one crying in the wilderness: Prepare the way for the Lord, make straight paths for Him.' John wore a garment of camel's hair.

Matthew 3:1-4

On confessing their sins they were baptised by John in the Jordan River.

'I baptise you in water . . . but coming after me is One mightier than I, whose sandals I am not worthy to remove.'

Matthew 3: 11
Luke 3: 16

At the peak of his ministry John baptised Jesus and proclaimed Him the Messiah.

Jesus came from Galilee to the Jordan River to John to be baptised by him . . . He went up immediately from the water, and behold, the heavens were opened, and He saw the Spirit of God descending like a dove and alighting upon Him: and lo, a voice from heaven saying: 'This is my beloved Son, with whom I am well pleased.'

Matthew 3: 13-17

The Jordan River

Honey in the making. Wild honey was part of John the Baptist's diet

JESUS was tempted in body, soul, and spirit

Then Jesus was led up by the Spirit into the wilderness to be tempted by the devil.

Matthew 4: 1

Jesus was tempted of the devil in the three areas of Body, Soul, and Spirit but He gloriously defeated His adversary in every round of the battle with the words, 'It is written'.

The three temptations were:
- Body: Make this stone bread.
- Soul: Throw yourself down (be spectacular!)
- Spirit: Fall down and worship me.

The sword of God's Word was wielded against man's foe, the devil, and victory was accomplished. This encounter was but the opening campaign. . . .

Greek Orthodox Monastery, built in 1874 on the Mount of Temptation at Jericho, usually recognised as the site of the event.

Then the devil taketh Him to the holy city, and set Him on the pinnacle of the temple, and said to Him: 'If you are the Son of God, throw yourself down.'

Part of the Jerusalem wall known as the pinnacle

Matthew 4: 5-6

The three temptations were countered by our Lord with the words of scripture:
Man shall not live by bread alone, but by every word that proceeds from the mouth of God.

Deuteronomy 8: 3

You shall not tempt the Lord your God.

Deuteronomy 6: 16

You shall worship the Lord your God and Him only shall you serve.   Deuteronomy 6: 13-14

JESUS GRACES A WEDDING

When the wine supply ran out the mother of Jesus said to Him: 'They have no wine'... Jesus said unto the servants: 'Fill the waterpots with water'. When the Governor of the feast tasted the water that Jesus had turned into wine, he called the bridegroom and said: 'You have kept the best wine until last.'
John 2: 3, 7, 10

This event was Christ's first miracle. Moses performed his first miracle in Egypt by turning water into blood—a miracle of judgment, but Jesus turned water into wine transforming the mundane to an enriching, sweet, joyous experience—a miracle of blessing. He willed instant chemical change. The process of years of grape juice maturing occurred in a moment. It has been well said: 'When the water saw the Creator, it blushed into beautiful wine.' The Lord Jesus came to satisfy all human life and to bring joy and blessing to Christian marriage.

Waterpots as used in Bible days

Model of temple courtyard, Holy Land Hotel

Jesus cleanses the temple

The Passover of the Jews was at hand, and Jesus went up to Jerusalem. In the temple He found those who were selling oxen and sheep and pigeons and the money-changers at their business. And making a whip of cords, He drove them out of the temple... and He told those who sold the pigeons: 'Take these things away; you shall not make my Father's house a house of trade.'
John 2: 13-16

A Personal interview

A section of the walled city of Jerusalem

While Jesus was in Jerusalem, *Nicodemus a ruler of the Jews came to Jesus by night* . . . Nicodemus was a Pharisee, which meant that he observed the Jewish laws to the minutest detail. He evidently wanted to make a private investigation of this great and unique teacher. In his first statement to Jesus he said: *'Rabbi, we know that you are a teacher come from God; for no one can do these signs unless God is with him.'* Jesus answered: *'Unless one is born anew, he cannot see the Kingdom of God.'*

John 3: 3

Some of the most sublime, well known and well loved statements of Jesus were made to Nicodemus.

Jesus said to Nicodemus: *'For God sent not His Son into the world to condemn the world; but that the world through Him might be saved. He that believeth on Him is not condemned; but he that believeth not is condemned already, because he hath not believed in the name of the only begotten Son of God.'*

John 3: 17-18

GOD so loved the world, that HE gave HIS only begotten SON, that whosoever believeth in HIM should not perish, but have Everlasting Life. John 3:16

A wind swept tree

Jesus said to Nicodemus: *'The wind blows where it wills, and you hear the sound of it, but you do not know whence it comes or whither it goes; so it is with every one who is born of the Spirit.'*

John 3: 8

Jesus must go through Samaria

Jacob's Well

Jacob's well was there. Jesus being weary with His journey sat on the well. There came a woman of Samaria to draw water. Jesus said to her: 'Give me a drink' . . . the woman said to Him: 'How is it that you, a Jew, ask a drink of me, a woman of Samaria?' . . . Jesus answered her: 'If you knew the gift of God, and who it is that is saying to you, Give me a drink, you would have asked Him, and He would have given you living water.'

John 4: 7-10

Water in abundance

Jesus said: *Everyone who drinks of this water shall thirst again, but whoever drinks of the water that I shall give him, will never thirst; the water that I shall give him will become in him a spring of water welling up to eternal life.'*   John 4: 14

JESUS, passing along by the Sea of Galilee

The Sea of Galilee

Mending nets — Sea of Galilee

And passing along by the Sea of Galilee, He saw Simon and Andrew the brother of Simon casting a net in the sea, for they were fishermen. And Jesus said to them: 'Follow me and I will make you to become fishers of men.' And immediately they left their nets and followed Him. And going on a little further, He saw James the son of Zebedee and John his brother, who were in the boat mending the nets. And immediately He called them . . . and they followed Him.

Mark 1: 16-20

Jesus spends a night in prayer

Mount Tabor

Jesus went into a mountain to pray and continued all night in prayer to God. When morning came, He called His disciples, and chose twelve of them whom He named apostles.

Luke 6:12,13

The appointment of His twelve disciples was of such importance that Jesus spent a night in prayer preceding their selection.

They left their nets and followed Him.

Matthew 4:20

Jesus travelled all through Galilee teaching in the Jewish synagogues, everywhere preaching the good news about the kingdom of heaven. And He healed every kind of sickness and disease. The report of His miracles spread far beyond the borders of Galilee.

Enormous crowds followed Him wherever He went; people from Galilee, and the Ten Cities, and Jerusalem, and from all over Judea, and even from across the Jordan River.

T.L.B. Matthew 4:23-25

Destination Capernaum

They went into Capernaum, and on the sabbath day He entered the synagogue and taught. They were astonished at His teaching. He taught them as one who had authority.

Mark 1: 21-22

Capernaum is called our Lord's own city.

Matthew 9: 1

It is located along the north-west shore of the Sea of Galilee, about four kilometres — 2½ miles — from where the Jordan River enters the sea. After He moved here from Nazareth, Jesus performed more miracles in this city than in any other. He cast out demons, and taught in the synagogue.

It was in Capernaum that Peter's wife's mother was healed, and Jairus's daughter was raised from the dead. It was probably here that Jesus met seven of the disciples after His resurrection.

Map of Galilee

Excavated millstone in Capernaum

A bread carrier in Jerusalem

Jesus said: *'Whoever causes one of these little ones who believe in me to lose his faith, it would be better for that man if a huge millstone were tied around his neck and he were thrown into the sea.'*

Mark 9: 42

Jesus said: *'I am the bread of life; he who comes to me shall never hunger, and he who believes in me shall never thirst.'*

John 6: 35

Reconstructed synagogue, Capernaum

In fulfilment of Christ's prophecy, the city faded out of existence. Today a partly reconstructed third century A.D. synagogue may be seen, also the remains of a fourth century A.D. church, and the lowest sections of walls of the township Jesus knew.

At Capernaum when the sun was setting, all those who had any that were sick with various diseases brought them to Him: and He laid His hands on every one of them and healed them.

Luke 4: 40

And you Capernaum, will you be exalted to heaven? You shall be brought down to Hades. For if the mighty works done in you had been done in Sodom it would have remained until this day. But I tell you it shall be more tolerable on the day of judgment for the land of Sodom than for you.

Matthew 11: 23-24

JESUS sat on the mountain and taught them saying . . .

Blessed are the poor in spirit, for theirs is the Kingdom of heaven.

Blessed are those who mourn, for they shall be comforted.

Blessed are the meek, for they shall inherit the earth.

Blessed are those who hunger and thirst for righteousness, for they shall be satisfied.

Blessed are the merciful, for they shall obtain mercy.

Blessed are the pure in heart, for they shall see God.

Blessed are the peacemakers, for they shall be called the sons of God.

Blessed are those who are persecuted for righteousness' sake, for theirs is the kingdom of heaven.
Matthew 5: 1-10

One side of the eight-sided Church of the Beatitudes. Each side represents a beatitude.

Spring flowers in Israel

Why are you anxious about clothing? Consider the lilies of the field, how they grow; they neither toil nor spin; yet I tell you, even Solomon in all his glory was not arrayed like one of these.
Matthew 6: 28-29

Seek ye first the kingdom of God, and His righteousness; and all these things shall be added unto you.
Matthew 6: 33

Ask, and it shall be given you; seek and ye shall find; knock and it shall be opened unto you.
Matthew 7: 7

Lay up for yourselves treasures in heaven, where neither moth nor rust doth corrupt, and where thieves do not break through and steal. For where your treasure is, there will your heart be also.
Matthew 6: 20-21

LORD, *to whom shall we go? You have the words of eternal life*   John 6:68

A section of Mount Zion as seen through the branches of a fig tree. The Bible sometimes uses the fig tree as an emblem of the nation of Israel.

Luke 21: 29-31

Israel now exports flowers to many countries of the world

Water lilies in Israel

Jesus said: *'Verily, verily, I say unto you, he that heareth my word, and believeth on Him that sent me, hath everlasting life, and shall not come into judgment; but is passed from death unto life.'*

John 5: 24

Everyone who acknowledges me before men, I will also acknowledge before my Father who is in heaven.   MLB Matthew 10: 32

Jesus said: *'Whatever you ask in my name, I will do it, that the Father may be glorified in the Son.'*

John 14: 13

And this is eternal life, that they may know you, the only true God, and Jesus Christ whom you have sent.

John 17:3

Jesus said, *''I give them eternal life, and they shall never perish, and no one shall snatch them out of my hand.''*

John 17:3

The grass withers and the flowers fall, but the word of the Lord endures for ever.

1 Peter 1:24,25

Look at the birds of the air; they neither sow nor reap nor gather into barns, and yet your heavenly Father keeps feeding them. Matthew 6: 26

There is a lad here who has five barley loaves and two fish. John 6: 9

By using these, Jesus performed a miracle in feeding five thousand people.

Enter by the narrow gate; for the gate is wide and the way is easy, that leads to destruction, and those who enter by it are many. The gate is narrow . . . that leads to life, and those who find it are few. Matthew 7: 13-14

A typical narrow gate in Jerusalem

A lad fishing in Galilee

On the slopes of the Mount of Olives

The Church of the Pater Noster, where the prayer Jesus taught His disciples is featured in sixty-two languages.

Mary Magdalene, from whom Jesus cast out seven demons, contributed, with the help of the other women, to the support of Jesus and His disciples. Luke 8: 2-3

Mary Magdalene was present at Christ's crucifixion, and at the sepulchre, and conversed with Jesus after His resurrection.

The Church of Mary Magdalene. This church with its seven golden domes was built by the Russian Czar, Alexander the Third.

Jesus taught in parables

Behold, there went out a sower to sow:

And it came to pass, as he sowed, some fell by the way side, and the fowls of the air came and devoured it up.

And some fell on stony ground, where it had not much earth; and immediately it sprang up, because it had no depth of earth:

But when the sun was up, it was scorched; and because it had no root, it withered away.

And some fell among thorns, and the thorns grew up, and choked it, and it yielded no fruit.

And other fell on good ground, and did yield fruit that sprang up and increased; and brought forth, some thirty, and some sixty, and some an hundred.

And His disciples asked Him, saying, 'What might this parable be?'

Now the parable is this: The seed is the word of God.

Those by the way side are they that hear; then cometh the devil, and taketh away the word out of their hearts, lest they should believe and be saved.

They on the rock are they, which, when they hear, receive the word with joy; and these have no root, which for a while believe, and in time of temptation fall away.

And that which fell among thorns are they, which, when they have heard, go forth, and are choked with cares and riches and pleasures of this life, and bring no fruit to perfection.

But that on the good ground are they which, having heard the word, keep it and bring forth fruit with patience.

Mark 4: 3-8
Luke 8: 11-15

An enemy hath sown tares among the wheat. Let them grow together until the harvest . . . and the reapers will gather the tares into bundles to burn them.

Matthew 13: 25

Bundles for burning

Some fell on stony ground

Jesus said: *'No one who puts his hand to the plough and looks back is fit for the kingdom of God.'*
Luke 9: 62

The Lord Jesus sent seventy others out two by two, into every town and place where He himself was about to come. And He said to them: 'The harvest truly is great, but the labourers are few; pray you therefore the Lord of the harvest to send out labourers into His harvest.' Luke 10: 1-2

JESUS the GREAT 'I AM'

An eastern shepherd leading his flock

Jesus said: *'I am the Good Shepherd.'*　　　John 10: 11

The shepherd character of our Lord portrays a picture of His care and protection for His flock. An eastern shepherd protects his sheep from harm and danger.

Jesus said: *'I am the door of the sheep.'* The shepherd would lie across the only entrance to the fold. He would be aware of any sheep tending to stray, and of any enemy molesting his sheep. He would call each sheep by name and they would follow him. Jesus as the Shepherd knows His sheep by name. He is always there to guide, protect, sustain and strengthen them. They enjoy belonging to the universal flock gathered from every tribe and tongue and nation.

Jesus said: *'Other sheep I have which are not of this fold, them also I must bring, so that there will be one flock encompassing Jew and Gentile.'*　　　John 10: 16

He is not only *the Good Shepherd, who gave His life for the sheep,*　　　John 10: 11
but He is *the Great Shepherd,* who lives for His sheep,
　　　Hebrews 13: 20,
and *the Chief Shepherd,* who will come again for His sheep and gather them into His eternal fold.　　　Peter 5: 4

I AM the Light of the world; he that followeth me shall not walk in darkness, but shall have the light of life.　　　John 8: 12

These words were spoken by the Lord prior to raising Lazarus from the dead.

When light shines through a prism we see a variety of colours. It needs the complete Bible to see the many glorious facets of Jesus Christ, the Light of the World. Because He is the Light, He said: *'I am the way.'* He lights the way, *'I am the truth,'* He illuminates the truth.

Wonderful evidence of Christ's eternal Deity is seen in the I AM's of John's Gospel. There never was a time when the Son did not exist. Before creation, before the sound of the wind in the trees, when all was solitude and starless night, the I AM of John's Gospel existed. Jesus said: *'Before Abraham was born, I AM.'* John 8: 58

This was the same phrase Jehovah used to reveal Himself in the Old Testament.

Jesus said, *'I am the bread of life; he who comes to Me shall not hunger, and he who believes in Me shall never thirst!*
I am the Living Bread which came down from heaven; if any one eats of this bread, he will live forever; and the bread which I shall give for the life of the world is my flesh! John 6:35,51

Who do men say that I AM?

Caesarea Philippi

JESUS was transfigured before them and His face did shine as the sun

refer Matthew 17:2

Now when Jesus came into the district of Caesarea Philippi, He asked His disciples: 'Who do men say that the Son of Man is?' and·they said: 'Some say John the Baptist, others say Elijah, and others, Jeremiah or one of the prophets.' He said to them: 'But who do you say that I am?' Simon Peter replied: 'You are the Christ, the Son of the living God.'
Matthew 16: 13-16

Mount Hermon, possible site of the transfiguration

A Church on Mount Tabor, one of the traditional sites of the transfiguration

I am the vine, you are the branches. He who abides in me, and I in him, he it is that bears much fruit for without ME you can do nothing John 15:5

Men do not put new wine into old wineskins Matthew 9:17

A Bedouin woman making yoghurt in a goat skin

Let the children come to me

People were bringing children to Him . . . and the disciples rebuked them but Jesus said: 'Let the little children come to me and hinder them not for to such belongs the kingdom of God.' And He took them in His arms and blessed them.

Mark 10: 13-14

His eye is on the sparrow

Feeding birds in Israel

Are not two sparrows sold for a penny? And not one of them will fall to the ground without your Father's will. But even the hairs of your head are all numbered. Fear not then. You are of more value than many sparrows.   Matthew 10: 29-31

Jesus drew near to Jericho and a blind man sat by the wayside begging . . . and he cried out saying: 'Jesus, Son of David, have mercy on me.' . . . Jesus asked him: 'What do you want me to do for you?' He said: 'Lord, let me receive my sight.' And Jesus said to him: 'Receive your sight, your faith has made you well.' And all the people gave praise to God.   Luke 18: 35-43

Zacchaeus was a chief tax collector in Jericho. He tried to see Jesus but was too short to see over the crowd. So he ran on ahead and climbed up into a sycamore tree to see Jesus. Jesus looked up and said to him: 'Zacchaeus, make haste and come down, for I must stay at your house today.' As a result of his repentance Jesus said to him: 'Today salvation has come to this house . . . for the Son of man came to seek and save the lost.'   Luke 19: 1-10

A sycamore tree in Jericho

A blind beggar at Jericho

Who is my neighbour?

And, behold, a certain lawyer stood up, and tempted Him, saying, 'Master, what shall I do to inherit eternal life?'

He said unto him, 'What is written in the law? How readest thou?'

And he answering said, 'Thou shalt love the Lord thy God with all thy heart, and with all thy soul, and with all thy strength, and with all thy mind; and thy neighbour as thyself.'

And He said unto him, 'Thou hast answered right: this do, and thou shalt live.'

But he, willing to justify himself, said unto Jesus, 'And who is my neighbour?'

And Jesus answering said, 'A certain man went down from Jerusalem to Jericho, and fell among thieves, which stripped him of his raiment, and wounded him, and departed, leaving him half dead.

And by chance there came down a certain priest that way: and when he saw him, he passed by on the other side.

And likewise a Levite, when he was at the place, came and looked on him, and passed by on the other side.

But a certain Samaritan, as he journeyed, came where he was: and when he saw him, he had compassion on him,

And went to him, and bound up his wounds, pouring in oil and wine, and set him on his own beast, and brought him to an inn, and took care of him.

And on the morrow when he departed, he took out two pence, and gave them to the host, and said unto him, "Take care of him; and whatsoever thou spendest more, when I come again, I will repay thee."

Which now of these three, thinkest thou, was neighbour unto him that fell among the thieves?'

And he said, 'He that shewed mercy on him.' Then said Jesus unto him, 'Go, and do thou likewise.'   Luke 10: 25-37

Referred to as the Good Samaritan Inn, approximately half way between Jerusalem and Jericho

Lost and found

In Luke 15, the Lord Jesus spoke of three lost things, The coin, the sheep, and the son. Although He was speaking to a large audience, He was showing them that the individual is precious to Him. The lost sinner could be likened to the coin, as an object of value; the sheep, as an object of care; the son, as an object of love.

There is joy in the presence of the angels of God over one sinner that repenteth.   Luke 15: 10

Destination Jerusalem

Jesus said: 'Behold we go up to Jerusalem; all things that are written by the prophets concerning the Son of man shall be accomplished. For He shall be delivered up to the Gentiles, to be mocked and shamefully treated and spat upon, and they will scourge Him and put Him to death, and the third day He shall rise again.'

Luke 18: 31-33

Six days before the Passover festival Jesus came to Bethany, where Lazarus lived whom He had raised from the dead. There a supper was given in His honour, at which Martha served, and Lazarus sat among the guests with Jesus. Then Mary brought a pound of very costly perfume, oil of pure nard, and anointed the feet of Jesus and wiped them with her hair, till the house was filled with the fragrance. At this, Judas Iscariot, a disciple of His—the one who was to betray Him— said: 'Why was this perfume not sold for thirty pounds and given to the poor?' He said this, not out of any care for the poor, but because he was a thief; he used to pilfer the money put into the common purse, which was in his charge. 'Leave her alone', said Jesus. 'Let her keep it till the day when she prepares for my burial; for you have the poor among you always, but you will not always have me.' Wherever this gospel is preached in the whole world, what she has done will be told in memory of her. John 12: 1-8, Matthew 26: 13

Church at Bethany to honour the memory of Mary, Martha and Lazarus
View of Jerusalem from a rooftop

*Behold
your King
is coming
sitting on
the colt of
an ass*
John 12:15

A procession from the Mount of Olives to Jerusalem is enacted by various denominations, on Palm Sunday

Jesus said: *'Go into the village opposite, where on entering you will find a colt tied, on which no one has ever yet sat. Untie it and bring it here.'* . . . *They brought it to Jesus, and throwing their garments on the colt, they sat Jesus upon it.*
Luke 19: 30-35

Others cut branches and spread them on the road, and the crowds that followed Him shouted: *'Hosanna in the highest.'* Matthew 21: 8-9

And some of the Pharisees in the multitude said: 'Master, rebuke your disciples.' He answered: 'I tell you, if these were silent, the very stones would cry out.' Luke 19: 39-40

Overlooking Jerusalem from the Church of Tears, where Jesus wept over Jerusalem and said: *O Jerusalem, Jerusalem, how often would I have gathered your children together as a hen gathers her brood under her wings, and you would not! Behold your house is forsaken and desolate. For I tell you, you will not see me again, until you say: 'Blessed is he who comes in the name of the Lord.'*

Matthew 23: 37-39

Note the Lord Jesus refers to the temple as *your house*. Early in His ministry He spoke of it as *My Father's house*. Jesus was filled with deep sorrow knowing their rejection of Him would lead to God's rejection of them nationally, and to the desolation of their temple.

What will be the sign of your return and the end of this age?

Mount of Olives from the Temple area

An artist's impression of Herod's Temple   MPS©

Jesus sat on the Mount of Olives opposite the Temple and His disciples asked Him privately: 'What will be the sign of your return and the end of this age?' Jesus answered: 'When you hear of wars and rumours of wars, be not terrified, for all these things must first take place, but the end is not yet. For nation shall rise against nation . . . and there shall be famines and pestilences, and earthquakes in various places; all these are the beginning of sorrows.'   Matthew 24: 3-8

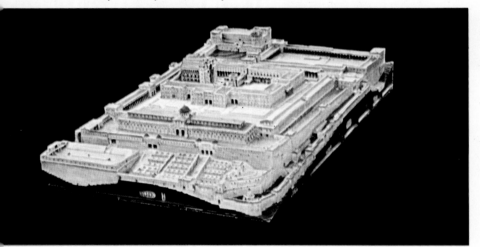

Jesus' disciples came to Him to show Him the buildings of the Temple, and He said unto them: 'See ye not all these things? Verily I say unto you, there shall not be left here one stone upon another that shall not be thrown down.'
  Matthew 24: 1-2

This was fulfilled in A.D. 70.

Jesus said: *'Jerusalem shall be trodden down by the Gentiles till the times of the Gentiles are fulfilled.'*   Luke 21: 24

This glad news of the kingdom must be proclaimed in all the world, to all nations, and then will the end come.   Matthew 24: 14

We are witnessing daily progressive fulfilment of this prophecy. Already the Bible in part or whole has been translated in over 1700 languages and dialects. A portion of the Bible is being completed in a new language every fourteen days. The scriptures have now been published in languages spoken by 97 per cent of the people of the world.

Monte Carlo, Monaco. It is from here that Trans World Radio beams the gospel to various countries of the world. This is one of a number of broadcasting stations used to herald the message of Jesus Christ

A reminder of the grandeur of the Roman Empire. The Christians suffered martyrdom and persecution during different periods of the Roman regime as Jesus had predicted in His Olivet discourse

THE SON OF MAN TO JUDGE THE NATIONS

Now when the Son of man comes in His glory, and with Him all the holy angels, then will He sit upon the throne of His glory, and before Him shall be gathered all the nations. And He will separate them one from another as a shepherd separates the sheep from the goats, and will put the sheep at His right hand, but the goats at the left. Then will the King say to those on His right hand: 'Come you blessed of my Father, inherit the Kingdom prepared for you from the foundation of the world. For I was hungry, and you gave me food; I was thirsty, and you gave me drink; I was a stranger and you made me welcome; I was naked and you clothed me; I was sick and you visited me; I was in prison and you came to me . . . Verily I say to you, inasmuch as you did it to one of the least of these my brethren, you did it to Me.'
Matthew 25: 31-46

Jesus said His coming would be sudden and unexpected. *Two women will be grinding at the mill, one shall be taken and the other left. Watch therefore, for you know not what hour your Lord will come.*
Matthew 24: 41-42

Lame beggar in Jerusalem

Excavated mills which two women would operate to grind grain

Jesus said, 'If any man thirst, let him come to me and drink.' John 7:37

A drink seller in Israel

Father, sanctify them through thy truth; thy word is truth John 17:17

After these words Jesus looked up to heaven and said:

'Father, the hour has come. Glorify thy Son, that the Son may glorify thee. For thou hast made him sovereign over all mankind, to give eternal life to all whom thou hast given him. This is eternal life: to know thee who alone art truly God, and Jesus Christ whom thou hast sent.

'I have glorified thee on earth by completing the work which thou gavest me to do; and now, Father, glorify me in thine own presence with the glory which I had with thee before the world began.

'I have made thy name known to the men whom thou didst give me out of the world. They were thine, thou gavest them to me, and they have obeyed thy command. Now they know that all thy gifts have come to me from thee; for I have taught them all that I learned from thee, and they have received it: they know with certainty that I came from thee; they have had faith to believe that thou didst send me.

'I pray for them; I am not praying for the world but for those whom thou hast given me, because they belong to thee.' John 17: 1-9

Jesus said: 'A good tree cannot bring forth evil fruit, nor can a bad tree bear good fruit, therefore by their fruits you shall know them.' Matthew 7: 18, 20

The Passover

Where will you have us go and prepare for you the passover? And He sent two of His disciples . . . and said: 'A man will show you a large upper room furnished and ready; there prepare for us.'
Mark 14: 12-15

Upper room, Jerusalem. Traditional site of the Last Supper

The ceremony of Feet Washing

If I then, your Lord and Master, have washed your feet, you ought also to wash one another's feet . . . If you know these things blessed are you if you do them.
John 13: 14-17

This act of love included washing the feet of one disciple who shortly afterwards would walk out of the room and betray the Lord, and those of another who later that evening would deny that he knew Him. Jesus said: *'I am among you as One who serves.'* His years of public ministry were marked by loving and unselfish service.

The silver tetradrachm is usually regarded as the coin Judas received, being the equivalent of the shekel
see Exodus 21:32

Judas went to the chief priests and said: 'What will you give me if I deliver Jesus to you?' They paid him thirty pieces of silver and from that moment he sought an opportunity to betray Him. After receiving the morsel, Judas immediately went out; and it was night.
Matthew 26: 14-16
John 13: 30

The LORD'S Supper

*The Lord Jesus on the night He was betrayed
took bread. When He had given thanks He broke
it, and said: 'This is my body which is for you.
Do this in remembrance of me.' In the same way
also the cup . . . saying: 'This cup is the new
covenant in my blood . . . For as often as you
drink this cup you proclaim the Lord's death
until He comes.'*　　　　I Corinthians 11: 23-26

Breaking the Passover Bread
(For further details regarding the passover plate see page 34)

*Peace I leave with you, my peace I give unto you . . . Let not
your heart be troubled.*　　　　John 14: 27

Behold your KING! But they crowned HIM with thorns

The Via Dolorosa

Jesus' agony in Gethsemane

*'My soul is exceeding sorrowful even unto death'
. . . Judas came to Jesus and said: 'Hail, Master,'
and kissed Him.*   Matthew 26: 38-49

*They seized Jesus and led Him away . . . to the
high priest's house.*   Luke 22: 54

From Gethsemane they would cross the Kidron
Valley and ascend to the high priest's house,
probably up these ancient excavated steps. Under-
neath the Via Dolorosa (the Way of the Cross) is
this pavement, probably the place where the
Roman soldiers mocked Jesus and crowned Him
with thorns.

The Garden of Gethsemane

*Excavated steps leading to the High Priest's
house*

When they came to a place called Calvary, there they crucified HIM Luke 23:33

The Church of the Holy Sepulchre. Six religious groups worship here; Latin (Roman), Eastern Orthodox, Armenian, Coptic, Syrian and Abyssinian.

Photographs of 'The Crucifixion' and 'The Resurrection' paintings are furnished through the courtesy of Forest Lawn Memorial Park, Glendale, California, where countless visitors see these great works of religious art and are inspired by their dramatic stories.

Thorns grown near Jerusalem

The Pavement. Possible site of the scourging of Jesus

The LORD is RISEN! Come see the place where the LORD lay

Looking down to the garden tomb, a possible burial place of Jesus

In the place where He was crucified there was a garden, and in the garden a new tomb where no one had ever been laid . . . They laid Jesus there.
John 19: 41-42

A large rolling stone similar to this covered the entrance to our Lord's tomb

On the first day of the week at early dawn, the women went to the tomb, taking spices which they had prepared. They asked each other, "Who will roll the stone away from the entrance of the tomb?" But when they looked up, they saw that the stone, which was very large, had been rolled away . . . An angel said to them, "He is not here. He is risen. Come and see the place where He lay."
Refer: Luke 24:1-3
Mark 16:2-4
Matthew 28:5,6

The angel said to the women, "Go, tell His disciples and Peter that He is going before you to Galilee; there you will see Him, as He told you." So they departed quickly from the tomb with fear and great joy, and ran to tell His disciples. And behold, Jesus met them . . . Mary Magdalene went and said to the disciples, "I have seen the Lord." Now the eleven disciples went to Galilee, to the mountain to which Jesus had directed them. And when they saw Him they worshipped Him.
Mark 16:7
Matthew 28:8,9; 6,17
John 20:18

The pulpit used at the Sunday services held outside the garden tomb

Photographs of 'The Crucifixion' and 'The Resurrection' paintings are furnished through the courtesy of Forest Lawn Memorial Park, Glendale, California, where countless visitors see these great works of religious art and are inspired by their dramatic stories.

With great power the apostles gave their testimony to the resurrection of the Lord Jesus. Peter, standing with the eleven, addressed them, "Men of Judea and all who dwell in Jerusalem, let this be known to you that the patriarch David both died and was buried, and his tomb is with us to this day. But this Jesus God raised up, and of that we all are witnesses."

Acts 4:33; 2:29,32.

Brothers, I want to remind you of the gospel . . . that Christ died for our sins according to the scriptures, that he was buried, that he was raised on the third day. If Christ has not been raised, your faith is futile; you are still in your sins. But Christ had indeed been raised from the dead, the first fruits of those who have fallen asleep.

1 Cor 15:1,3,4,17,20.

Looking out to the garden from the empty tomb.

Jesus Himself drew near and went with them

The same day that Jesus rose from the dead two of His followers were walking to the village of Emmaus about seven miles from Jerusalem . . . Jesus Himself drew near and went with them . . . And beginning with Moses and all the prophets, He interpreted to them in all the Scriptures the things concerning Himself. . . . They said to each other: 'Did not our hearts burn within us as He talked with us by the way?' Luke 24: 13-32

The road to Emmaus

By the Western Wall. Great love and respect are shown for the writings of Moses

Jesus said: 'Everything written about me in the law of Moses and the prophets and the Psalms must be fulfilled.' Luke 24: 44

The RISEN CHRIST and the DISCIPLES reunite at GALILEE

Peter said: 'I am going fishing.' The other disciples said: 'We will go with you.' . . . That night they caught nothing. Just as day was breaking, Jesus stood on the beach . . . He said to them: 'Cast the net on the right side of the boat.' . . . They hauled the net ashore, full of large fish—one hundred and fifty-three of them . . . John said: 'It is the Lord.'
They ate fish and bread together for breakfast.
This was the third time that Jesus was revealed to the disciples after He was raised from the dead.
John 21: 3-14

Fishermen on the Sea of Galilee

When they had finished breakfast, Jesus said to Simon Peter: 'Simon, son of John, do you love me more than these?' He said to Him: 'Yes, Lord; you know that I love you.' He said to him: 'Feed my lambs.' A second time He said to him: 'Simon, son of John, do you love me?' He said to Him: 'Yes, Lord; you know that I love you.' He said to him: 'Tend my sheep.' He said to him the third time: 'Simon, son of John, do you love me?' Peter was grieved because He said to him the third time, Do you love me? And he said to Him: 'Lord, you know everything; you know that I love you.' Jesus said to him: 'Feed my sheep.'
John 21: 15-17

Then He led them out as far as Bethany [the Mount of Olives].
And lifting up His hands He blessed them . . . and while He
blessed them He was carried up into heaven . . . Luke 24: 50-52
And while they were gazing into heaven as He went, behold,
two men stood by them in white robes, and said: 'Men of
Galilee, why do you stand looking into heaven? This Jesus
who was taken up from you into heaven, will come in the
same way as you saw Him go into heaven.' Acts 1: 10-11

The Mount of Olives is at least 76 metres — 250 feet — higher
than the temple area; it is about 1.6 kilometres — one mile —
in length, and 836 metres — 2743 feet — above sea level.

David ascended the Mount of Olives, weeping as he went,
when he was fleeing from his son Absalom. II Samuel 15: 30
Jesus commenced His Palm Sunday walk from here. His
discourse about future events was given here. Gethsemane,
where He agonised in prayer, is part of the Mount of Olives.

WHICH CHRIST ASCENDED

The Mount of Olives in prophecy:
And the glory of the Lord went up from the midst of the city, and stood upon the mountain which is on the east side of the city.
Ezekiel 11: 23

Rabbi Janna says in the Midrash that the Shechinah, or Divine Presence, after leaving Jerusalem, dwelt for three and one half years on the Mount of Olives to see if the Jews would repent; then He departed. The Mount of Olives will be the place to which the Lord Jesus will return and His glory will be seen by all. Every time the Lord Jesus penetrates our atmosphere, God issues a command for all the angels to worship Him. It happened at Bethlehem when the heavenly hosts said: *'Glory to God in the highest.'* It will happen when God brings His first begotten again into the world. He says: *'Let all the angels of God worship Him.'*
Hebrews 1: 6
Then the Lord your God will come, and all the holy ones with Him.
Zechariah 14: 5

PENTECOST: The Church is Born

The Mount of Olives

It was here that Jesus said to His disciples prior to His ascension: *'You shall receive power when the Holy Spirit is come upon you; and you shall be my witnesses in Jerusalem and in all Judea and Samaria and the uttermost part of the earth.'*

Acts 1: 8

The Church was born on the day of Pentecost when about 120 believers were baptised with the Holy Spirit. Units were united into the Body of Christ. The initial establishment of the Church in Jerusalem led to its development throughout Asia, to Rome and to the uttermost parts of the earth. It commenced with thousands of Jewish believers and expanded to embrace Gentiles of every tribe and tongue and nation. Christ's ascension completed His work on earth. In heaven, He continues His work through and for the Church.

STEPHEN MARTYRED FOR HIS FAITH

Stephen, the first Christian martyr, was stoned to death outside the Jerusalem wall, probably near the Damascus Gate

Left: One of the Jerusalem gates, usually referred to as the Lion's Gate

The Samaritans respond

Philip went down to a city of Samaria and proclaimed Christ. Multitudes with one accord gave heed to what was said.

Acts 8: 5-6

So the church throughout all Judea and Galilee and Samaria was built up, and walking in the fear of the Lord and in the comfort of the Holy Spirit, it was multiplied.

Acts 9: 31

Samaritans with ancient scroll of the Pentateuch

The Samaritans still sacrifice a lamb each year at Passover

PAUL'S DRAMATIC CONVERSION

Saul, still breathing threats and murder against the disciples of the Lord, went to the high priest and asked him for letters to the synagogues at Damascus, so that if he found any belonging to the Way . . . he might bring them bound to Jerusalem. As he approached Damascus . . . suddenly a light from heaven flashed about him, he fell to the ground and heard a voice saying to him: 'Saul, Saul, why do you persecute me?' And he said: 'Who are you, Lord?' He said: 'I am Jesus, whom you are persecuting, but rise and enter the city and you will be told what to do.' Saul was blind when he arose from the ground.

The Lord said to Ananias: 'Go to the street called Straight, and inquire in the house of Judas for a man of Tarsus named Saul, for behold he is praying . . . he is a chosen instrument of mine to carry my name before the Gentiles, and Kings, and the Sons of Israel.' Saul regained his sight and was baptised . . . and immediately in the synagogues he proclaimed Jesus, saying: 'He is the Son of God.'

Acts 9: 1-20

The street called Straight, Damascus

The land jutting out to sea is ancient Joppa. Its continuous history goes back more than 5000 years

CORNELIUS, THE FIRST GENTILE TO EMBRACE CHRISTIANITY

Cornelius was an Italian army officer, who in spite of his pagan background knew how to pray and share his pay with God's people. As always, God meets the need of a sincere seeking soul. God sent him a messenger who said: *'Send men to Joppa, and bring Peter. He is lodging with Simon, a tanner, whose house is by the seaside.'*

Acts 10: 5-6

Peter went up to the housetop to pray. Acts 10: 9 He had a vision which revealed to him that God had no favourites, but *anybody of any nationality who fears God is acceptable to Him.* Acts 10: 35

Peter went down from the rooftop to greet three men from Caesarea. They requested him to go with them to their master's home. His name was Cornelius, a Roman centurion.

Joppa is called Jaffa today. Some say it was named after Japheth, the son of Noah, who established the town after the flood. The cedars of Lebanon were floated to Joppa for Solomon's temple. II Chronicles 2: 16

Jonah sailed from Joppa to Tarsish. Jonah 1: 3

At Joppa, Dorcas was raised from the dead.

Acts 9: 36-42

Steps leading to the rooftop of the house reputed to be that of Simon the tanner

Caesarea

Here at Caesarea, Peter presented the good news about Christ Jesus the Saviour to the Roman centurion Cornelius, who became the first Gentile to embrace Christianity. All of the guests in his house at the time also believed.

Acts 10: 34-48

Caesarea was founded by Herod the Great in approximately 22 B.C. It was the Roman capital of Judea for over 400 years. It was the home of Philip the Evangelist. Herod was smitten by an angel and died there. Paul visited Caesarea many times and was imprisoned there for two years, then sailed to Rome.

PAUL AND BARNABAS SAIL TO CYPRUS

The Holy Spirit said: 'Set apart for me Barnabas and Saul for the work to which I have called them' . . . They laid their hands on them and sent them . . . to Cyprus . . . They proclaimed the word of God in the synagogues of the Jews . . . The proconsul believed . . . for he was astonished at the teaching of the Lord.

Acts 13: 2-12

Aqueduct at Caesarea bringing the water from the Carmel Ranges

An underground meeting place at Paphos, Cyprus

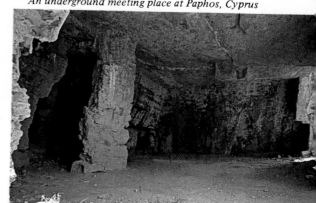

*They that were scattered abroad (because of the persecution) wen[t]
everywhere preaching the word* Acts 8:4-11

It seems that the Apostles remained in Jerusalem while the ordinary folk went everywhere 'gossiping' the gospel. The persecution of the Christians gave renewed impetus to the spreading of the gospel. God used ordinary people in extraordinary ways.

A section of the Greek coast

Peter freed from Jerusalem prison in night time miracle

To please the Jewish leaders, King Herod arrested Peter during the Passover celebration and imprisoned him, placing him under the guard of sixteen soldiers. His intention was to deliver Peter to the Jews for execution after the Passover. But earnest prayer was going up to God from the Church for his safety all the time he was in prison. *The night before he was to be executed, he was asleep, double-chained between two soldiers with others standing guard before the prison gate, when suddenly there was a light in the cell and an angel of the Lord stood beside Peter and said: 'Quick, get up!' And the chains fell off his wrists. Then the angel told him: 'Get dressed and put on your shoes and put on your coat and follow me.' So Peter left the cell, following the angel. But all the time he thought it was a dream or vision, and did not believe it was really happening. They passed the first and second cell blocks and came to the iron gate to the street, and this opened to them of its own accord. So they passed through and walked along together, and then the angel left him. Peter finally realised what had happened. 'It's really true,' he said to himself. 'The Lord has sent His angel and saved me from Herod and from what the Jews were hoping to do to me.'*

TLB Acts 12: 6-11

Night falls over Jerusalem

Come over to Macedonia and help us Acts 16:9

Kavalla (ancient Neapolis) where Paul first set foot in Europe

We came with a straight course to Neapolis and from there to Philippi which is the leading city in the district of Macedonia.   Acts 16: 12

Paul's arrival in Europe some twenty years after the church commenced at Pentecost was a very strategic move in the spread of the Gospel. He took up residence in the Macedonian capital of Philippi. More often than not Paul settled in main centres; places from which the roads, and the message, would go in all directions. Rome little realised that Paul's advancement into one of their frontier cities was another step towards weakening her influence and changing the world's history.

Paul and Timothy, servants of Jesus Christ, to all the saints in Christ Jesus at Philippi . . . "I thank my God for every remembrance of you. It is my prayer . . . that you may approve what is excellent . . . being filled with the fruits of righteousness which come through Jesus Christ to the glory and praise of God."

Philippians 1:1,3,9-11

Midnight miracle at Philippi prison

Inscription on the prison wall at Philippi, the traditional site of the imprisonment of Paul and Silas

Ruins of ancient Philippi

At Philippi, Paul accompanied by Silas proclaimed the way of salvation. They were arrested, tried, and cast into prison. *And about midnight Paul and Silas were praying and singing hymns to God . . . and suddenly there was a great earthquake, so that the foundations of the prison were shaken; and immediately all the doors were opened and everyone's fetters were unfastened . . . Trembling with fear the jailor fell down before Paul and Silas and brought them out and said: 'Sirs, what must I do to be saved?' and they said: 'Believe on the Lord Jesus Christ and thou shalt be saved.'*

Acts 16: 25-31

At Thessalonica *They turned to God from idols to serve the true*

A touch of old and new at Thessalonica

The remains of the arch of Galerius in Thessalonica

Byzantine church at Thessalonica, honouring the memory of Paul

*and living God and
to wait for His Son
from heaven, whom He
raised from the dead,
even Jesus, who delivers
us from the wrath to
come*

I Thessalonians 1:9, 10

In his letters to the church at Thessalonica, Paul
highlights in every chapter the coming again
of Jesus Christ.

*They came to Thessalonica, where there was a
synagogue of the Jews. And Paul went in, as was
his custom, for three sabbath days and reasoned
with them out of the scriptures explaining and
proving that it was necessary for the Christ to
suffer and to rise from the dead, and some of
them believed, as did a great many of the devout
Greeks, and not a few of the leading women.*

Acts 17: 1-4

*The oldest synagogue in Melbourne, Australia, is built
on traditional lines. The upstairs area is for the women.
The holy ark at the far end holds scrolls of the Scripture.
The lectern, from which the scrolls are read, is shown in
the foreground*

The Areopagus, or Mars Hill. This hill looking east to the Acropolis was the meeting place of the council of elders and the court of justice. Paul may have preached here of the unknown God

Paul's spirit was provoked within him as he saw the city was full of idols. Acts 17: 16

Paul, standing in the middle of the Areopagus said: 'Men of Athens, I perceive that in every way you are very religious. For as I passed along, and observed the objects of your worship, I found also an altar with this inscription "To an unknown God". What therefore you worship as unknown, this I proclaim to you . . . The times of ignorance God overlooked, but now He commands all men everywhere to repent, because He has fixed a day on which He will judge the world in righteousness by that man whom He has appointed, and of this He has given assurance to all men by raising Him from the dead.' Acts 17: 22-31

The Acropolis, Athens

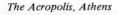

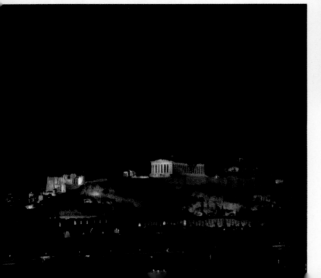

Paul went through the region of Galatia, strengthening all the disciples Acts 16:5, 6

Byzantine Church at Iconium

Mosque at Iconium, Galatia

General view of Ankara, Galatia

The Son of God loved me, and gave Himself for me.   Galatians 2: 20

Paul and Barnabas entered the synagogue at Iconium, and a great company believed both of Jews and Greeks.
                                                                  Acts 14: 1

Paul left Athens and went to Corinth Acts 18:1

A section of modern Corinth, including areas of ancient Corinth which have been excavated (foreground).

The Corinth Canal opened in 1893. The idea was first conceived by Nero in A.D. 67. It links the Aegean Sea and the Adriatic Sea. Through its harbours poured in the world's commerce. The vices of east and west met at Corinth.

And Paul stayed in Corinth eighteen months teaching the Word of God.   Acts 18: 11

God is able to make all grace abound toward you: that ye always having all sufficiency in all things, may abound in every good work: . . . being enriched in every thing to all bountifulness, which causeth through us thanksgiving to God.
                                    II Corinthians 9: 8-11

And although I have all faith, so that I could move mountains, and have not love, I am nothing   I Corinthians 13:2

Love is patient and kind; love is not jealous or boastful; it is not arrogant or rude. Love does not insist on its own way; it is not irritable or resentful; it does not rejoice at wrong, but rejoices in the right. Love bears all things, believes all things, hopes all things, endures all things.

Love never ends; as for prophecies, they will pass away; as for tongues, they will cease; as for knowledge, it will pass away. For our knowledge is imperfect and our prophecy is imperfect; but when the perfect comes, the imperfect will pass away. When I was a child, I spoke like a child, I thought like a child, I reasoned like a child; when I became a man, I gave up childish ways. For now we see in a mirror dimly, but then face to face. Now I know in part; then I shall understand fully, even as I have been fully understood. So faith, hope, love abide, these three; but the greatest of these is love.

I Corinthians 13: 4-13

The remains of the temple of Apollo with the Acrocorinth in the background

Paul travelled through Turkey and arrived at Ephesus Acts 19:1

A marble street of Ephesus

And the elders from Ephesus came to Paul at Miletus . . . and when he had spoken to them, he knelt down and prayed with them. And they all wept and embraced Paul . . . sorrowing . . . because they should see his face no more.
Acts 20: 17-18, 36-38

Ephesus was famous for its trade, its games, its temple and its theatre. A long marble street flanked by stately columns went from the theatre to the harbour. Now the harbour is a desolate swamp. After the felling of the trees on the surrounding hillside the topsoil filled the harbour. The church died with the city.

One of Paul's prayers for the Christians at Ephesus: *'For this reason I bow my knees before the Father, from whom every family in heaven and on earth is named, that according to the riches of His glory He may grant you to be strengthened with might through His Spirit in the inner man, and that Christ may dwell in your hearts through faith; that you, being rooted and grounded in love, may have power to comprehend with all the saints what is the breadth and length and height and depth, and to know the love of Christ which surpasses knowledge, that you may be filled with all the fulness of God. Now to Him who by the power at work within us is able to do far more abundantly than all that we ask or think, to Him be glory in the church and in Christ Jesus to all generations for ever and ever.' Amen.*
Ephesians 3: 14-21

The Miletus Market Gate (East Berlin Museum)

A Baptistry at Ephesus

I will stay in Ephesus until Pentecost I Corinthians 16:8

Paul remained at Ephesus for at least two and a half years. He worked at his trade of tent making each morning, and taught in the school of Tyrannus each afternoon. This was so effective that every resident of Asia heard the word of the Lord; both Jews and Greeks.

Acts 19: 10

Demetrius, a silversmith, who made shrines of Artemis . . . gathered together workmen of like occupation, and said: 'Men, you know that from this business we have our wealth, and not only at Ephesus but almost throughout all of Asia this Paul has persuaded a considerable number of people, saying that gods made with hands are not gods. And there is danger that this trade of ours . . . of making silver shrines of Diana . . . may come into disrepute, and also that the temple of the great goddess Diana should be despised' . . . When they heard this they were enraged; and they rushed together into the theatre dragging with them Gaius and Aristarchus, Paul's companions . . . they cried out . . . for about two hours: 'Great is Diana of the Ephesians.'

Acts 19: 24-34

Diana of the Ephesians

The Temple of Artemis at Ephesus, one of the seven wonders of the ancient world, was close to the harbour's edge. Today just one column stands.

The theatre at Ephesus seats 24 000 people

We sailed straight to Cos, and the next day to Rhodes Acts 21:1

Ruins of the temple of the Greek goddess Athena

Bay of Paul, Rhodes

A small section of the large island of Crete

Titus, my true child
in the common faith . . .
I left you in Crete,
that you might set
in order the things
that are wanting,
and ordain elders
in every city.

Titus 1: 4-5

Epaphras, from your city of Colossee . . . worked hard for you and for those in Laodicea and in Hierapolis Colossians 4:12, 13

Because of the unique calcium-formed cliffs at Hierapolis, it is sometimes called Cotton Castle. Hot thermal water cascades over the cliffs.

Three cities lay in the one valley, Colosse, Laodicea and Hierapolis. They probably shared Paul's letters as well as John's.

To the Jewish Christians . . . throughout . . . Asia . . . Cappadocia I Peter 1:1

Part of underground Cappadocia Church at Cappadocia

Blessed be the God and Father of our Lord Jesus Christ which according to His abundant mercy hath begotten us unto a living hope by the resurrection of Jesus Christ from the dead, to an inheritance incorruptible, and undefiled, and that fadeth not away, reserved in heaven for you.
I Peter 1: 3-4

The trial of your faith, being much more precious than of gold that perisheth, though it be tried with fire, might be found unto praise and honour and glory at the appearing of Jesus Christ, whom having not seen, you love; in whom, though now you see Him not, yet believing, you rejoice with joy unspeakable and full of glory; receiving the end of your faith, even the salvation of your souls.
1 Peter 1:7-9

Antioch

A section of the island of Malta

Paul wrote, *I hope to see you in passing as I go to Spain.*
Romans 15: 24

A town on the Spanish coast

Antioch, where Paul and his company entered the synagogue on the sabbath day. As part of his message, Paul made this great statement: *'Be it known unto you that through Jesus Christ is preached unto you the forgiveness of sins, and by Him all that believe are justified from all things, from which you could not be justified by the law of Moses.'*
Acts 13: 38-39

PAUL WINTERS AT MALTA

Paul sailed from Caesarea to Italy as a prisoner, to be tried before Caesar. They called at various ports on the way until they arrived at Myra. There, Paul, the other prisoners, and the passengers were transferred to a larger ship. After calling at the island of Crete, they set sail, against the advice of Paul. Ultimately they were shipwrecked off the coast of Malta. God used Paul during his three months there in a wonderful healing ministry to the islanders. They then set sail again for Italy.
see Acts 28, 29

At Rome, Paul stayed in his rented house, guarded by a soldier

Acts 28:16-31

Paul was able to use his time to advantage during his two years in Rome because of the special privileges given him as a prisoner awaiting trial. He was able to *welcome all who came to him, preaching the Kingdom of God and teaching about the Lord Jesus Christ quite openly and unhindered.*

Acts 28: 30-31

The Colosseum in Rome. It held 45 000 spectators

Because of the persecution and martyrdom the Christians were undergoing in Rome, one can imagine the impact of Paul's letter to them. In chapter eight he writes, *I consider that the sufferings of this present time are not worth comparing with the glory to be revealed to us. For I am persuaded that neither death, nor life, nor angels, nor principalities, nor powers, nor things present, nor things to come, nor height, nor depth, nor any other creature, shall separate us from the love of God, which is in Christ Jesus our Lord.*

Romans 8: 18, 38-39

This arch was built to commemorate Titus, especially his capture of Jerusalem in A.D. 70

This freize inside the arch depicts the triumphal procession when the soldiers returned to Rome. Note the seven branched candlestick of pure gold and the trumpets from the temple in Jerusalem

142

A letter to the seven churches

The island of Patmos, where John wrote the Revelation of Jesus Christ, is almost severed in two. It is 12.87 kilometres – 8 miles – long, and 8 kilometres – 5 miles – wide

I, John . . . was on the island called Patmos for the word of God and the testimony of Jesus Christ . . . Revelation 1: 9

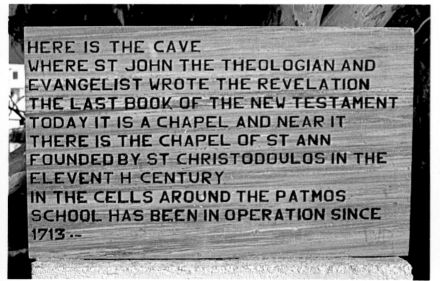

I turned and saw seven golden lampstands, and in the midst of the lampstands, one like unto the Son of man . . . Revelation 1: 12-13

The letters to the seven churches contain the only words the Lord Jesus spoke directly to the church on earth. There were probably churches in every one of the 230 provinces of Asia. These seven lay on a strategic circular route, making it convenient to distribute the letters. These seven centres would receive a message suitable to all churches, both then, and now.

To the church in Ephesus

"I know your works, your toil and your patient endurance , . . I know you are enduring patiently and bearing up for my name's sake, and you have not grown weary. But I have this against you, that you have abandoned the love you had at first. Remember then from what you have fallen, repent and do the works you did at first. If not, I will come to you and remove your lampstand from its place, unless you repent." Revelation 2:2-5

Sections of the ruins at Ephesus

To the church in Smyrna

Izmir (ancient Smyrna) is a natural seaport. When the harbour at Ephesus silted up, business was transferred to Smyrna. It is now the third largest city in Turkey, which was once known as Asia.

Smyrna once died as a city and later came alive again. John encouraged the persecuted Christians there with these words; *"This message is from Him who is the First and the Last, who died and came back to life. 'I know your tribulation and your poverty (but you are rich) . . . Do not fear what you are about to suffer . . . Be faithful unto death, and I will give you the crown of life'."*
Revelation 2:8-10

Smyrna

To the church in Pergamum

The huge granite hill of Pergamum rises 304.8 metres — 1000 feet — above the plain. The ruins on top pinpoint the library with its 200 000 books, its theatres and its various gymnasiums for boys, youth and the gentry.

I know your works, your love and faith and service and patient endurance. Your recent works exceed your first ones, but I have this against you, that you tolerate the woman Jezebel . . . who is beguiling my servants to practise immorality and to eat food sacrificed to idols. Revelation 2: 19-20

I know where you dwell, where Satan's throne is.
Revelation 2: 13

Some commentators suggest that Satan's throne refers to the great altar of Zeus, once situated on this site.

Reconstructed Pergamum temple, Pergamon Museum, East Berlin

To him who conquers . . . I will give a white stone with a new name on it. Revelation 2: 17

A Greek jury would vote with black or white stones; black for guilty, white for acquittal, but possibly the thought behind our Lord's promise of a white stone with a new name on it gets its setting from the fortress of Pergamum. All the local stone was black basalt and was quite unsuitable for inscriptions. White marble was imported to inscribe the noble deeds of an honoured person. The promise by our Lord of a new name on a white stone proves how precious the individual is to the Lord.

The Roman sword stood for the power of life or death over all the inhabitants. The Lord Jesus reminds the church at Pergamum that He is the One who has the sharp two-edged sword. His judgments will ultimately overrule the false verdicts of the human court.

Sword monument in Turkey

Models of the temples at Pergamum. Pergamon Museum, East Berlin

Old and new at Thyatira

To the church in Thyatira

There were more trade guilds at Thyatira than at any other city. The guilds gave patronage to the pagan gods, making it difficult for Christian tradesmen. Jezebel offered prosperity at the price of pagan practices. She seduced Christ's servants to sin.

Thyatira was famous for its purple dyes. There were guilds for tanners, dyers, woollen and linen workers etc. Scores of Christians died rather than compromise with the impure gaieties of the guilds.

To the overcomer I will give power over the nations, and he shall rule with a rod of iron, as when pottery is broken in pieces.
Revelation 2: 26-27

Ancient Sardis was situated on this range

To the church in Sardis

Sardis. You have the name of being alive, and you are dead. Awake, and strengthen what remains . . . I will come like a thief and you will not know at what hour I will come upon you.
Revelation 3: 1-3

Sardis stood on this impregnable lookout 457.5 metres — 1500 feet — above the plain. Cyrus's men climbed the cliff face at night when the guards were asleep. They came like a thief in the night. *He who conquers will walk with me in white.* Victory was possible even in a city that suffered defeat.
Revelation 3: 4

To the church in Philadelphia

Philadelphia as it appears today

Temple pillars at Jerash, Jordan

Because you have kept My word of patient endurance, I will keep you from the hour of trial which is coming on the whole world, to try those who dwell upon the earth. Notice the glorious promise is to keep them from, and not in, the hour of trial.

Revelation 3: 10

Philadelphia suffered severe earthquakes. No temple pillars such as these could stand, because of the earth's shaky movements. Our Lord says to the Christians at Philadelphia: *'I will make you a pillar in the temple of my God.'*

Revelation 3: 12

To the church in Laodicea

Looking over the valley of Laodicea

Laodicea. I know your works, you are neither cold nor hot . . . because you are lukewarm . . . I will spew you out of my mouth. For you say, I am rich, I have prospered, and I need nothing; not knowing that you are wretched, pitiable, poor, blind and naked. I council you to buy from me gold refined by fire . . . and white garments to clothe you . . . and salve to annoint your eyes, that you may see, so be zealous (enthusiastic) and repent.   Revelation 3: 15-19

Laodicea exported eye salve to many parts of the world, but the Christians were unaware of their own spiritual blindness.

Laodicea's water supply was channelled through this dual pipeline. It carried thick calcium impurities. If a visitor drank the lukewarm water it would make him vomit. *You are lukewarm, I will spew you out of my mouth.*
    Revelation 3: 16

The lukewarm water in the village adjacent to Laodicea is very beneficial to the eyes. Note the calcium layer on the ruins.

Holman Hunt's painting 'The Light of the World' as seen in St Paul's Cathedral, London

Behold I stand at the door and knock, if any man hear my voice, and open the door, I will come in to Him, and will sup with him, and he with me.

Revelation 3: 20

The Lord Jesus Christ is seen in the seven churches as the one who:
Walks in the midst of the seven candlesticks,
Has the seven stars in His right hand,
Is the first and the last,
Was dead and is alive,
Has eyes like unto a flame of fire,
Has the sharp two edged sword,
Has feet like fine brass,
Has the seven spirits of God,
Has the key of David,
Is the Amen, the faithful and true witness,
Is the beginning of the creation of God.

Our bountiful Lord is sufficient for every need of every church.

Hold fast 'Until I come'.

Wonderful promises of future glory.
'Tree of life in the midst of the paradise of God',
'Deliverance from the hurt of the second death',
The joy of receiving the 'hidden manna',
The 'white stone' with a new name written on it,
The privilege of ruling with the eternal King,
The glory of walking with the Lord in white garments,
The honour of being the 'pillars in the temple of God',
The favour of dining at the table of the Lord.

The following paragraph written in 1854 contains excerpts from Ruskin's description of Holman Hunt's painting.
'On the left hand side is the door of the human soul; its bars and nails are rusty, the creeping ivy shows it has never been opened. Christ approaches it in the night-time. The crown of gold interwoven with the crown of thorns is bearing soft leaves for the healing of the nations. He bears with Him a twofold light; first, the light of conscience which displays our sin, and afterwards the light of peace, the hope of salvation.'

All that remains of the water distribution tower at Laodicea. Water from the pipe lines, shown on previous page, was distributed from the tower throughout the city. Note the white cliffs in the background. These are shown in detail on page 139.

150

ISRAEL TODAY!

I will bring back the exiles and they shall build the waste cities, and live in them again

Amos 9:14

High rise apartments in Jerusalem. It is a much larger city today than in the days of Christ

The verses quoted on this and the following three pages seem to have a partial fulfilment today. The Messianic age will see their complete fulfilment.

God's providential hand has been seen in miracle after miracle since the State of Israel was formed in 1948. These miracles are either national history or current events.

Israel is a nation of miracles. Jews have returned from over 100 countries; speaking eighty different languages, yet they are merging together into a strong nation. The revival of Hebrew, which has been a dead conversational language for 2000 years, has helped to unite the Israelis in spite of their varying backgrounds.

Ezekiel's prophecy of the Valley of Dry Bones is being fulfilled in correct sequence.　　Ezekiel 37

The 'Dry Bones' are being resurrected from many Gentile countries; and the miracle of restored nationhood, after two thousand years, is the forerunner of the Messianic age when God's Spirit will indwell them and they will become the spiritual force that God ordained.

A corner of modern Haifa. Note the memorial boat which brought exiles from Europe

And it shall come to pass in that day the Lord shall set His hand a second time to recover the remnant of His people . . . and will gather the dispersed from the four corners of the earth.
Isaiah 11:11,12

A section of the students' quarters at the Beersheba University

151

Blossoming as the rose

Israel has a great variety of vegetation within a comparatively small area due to the different features of its tropical, sub-tropical, and temperate zones. There are coastal plains and snow-capped mountains, lush valleys and deserts, and the lowest rift valley in the world. There are approximately 3000 different species of plants.

The land that was rocky and barren for the last 1900 years is now so productive, that millions of dollars worth of fruit, vegetables and cut flowers are being exported annually.

But you, O mountains of Israel, shall shoot forth your branches, and yield your fruit to my people Israel for they will soon come home. Ezekiel 36: 8

The Red Sea abounds with exotic marine life. Colourful fish are a vivid contrast to the myriad hues of magnificent coral.

The wilderness and the solitary place shall be glad for them; and the desert shall blossom as the rose. It shall blossom abundantly, and rejoice even with joy and singing; the glory of Lebanon shall be given unto it, the excellency of Carmel and Sharon, they shall see the glory of the Lord, and the excellence of our God.

Isaiah 35: 1-2

This prophecy has yet to be completely fulfilled.

Some of Israel's rich variety of fruit and vegetables

Market day in Israel

But despite all they have done . . . I will remember my promise to their ancestors; then will the Lord be jealous for the land and will pity His people, and will send corn and wine and oil.

Joel 2: 18-19
see Leviticus 26:44-45

Cotton harvester, Israel

Birds in abundance

The Ospray   see Leviticus 11: 13

The Pied Kingfisher

The Hoopoe is now plentiful and delights to flirt its fine crown
(Painting: Betsy Lew)

Bird life in Israel is rapidly increasing. Some migratory birds, that dropped down in Israel for a rest, have now taken up residence there. The reaforrestation program with its increase of over one hundred million trees must surely encourage bird life. Birds that were once very rare are now in home gardens. One bird watcher from Australia saw one hundred and ten new types of birds in Israel. When a flock of pelicans cleaned out a whole pond of marketable fish, the bird society paid the kibbutz their market value immediately. Quail are in abundance and rise from underfoot as you walk through rough grass. Vultures have a part in Bible prophecy, and are becoming prolific in Israel today.

The LORD is building Jerusalem, and is gathering the exiles of Israel Psalm 147:2

View from the wall of the old city of Jerusalem near Herod's Gate. The new city is in the distance

Thus says the Lord: 'I will return to Zion, and will dwell in the midst of Jerusalem, and Jerusalem shall be called the faithful city.' Zechariah 8: 3

A prophecy yet to be fulfilled.

Our feet shall stand within your gates, O Jerusalem!
Psalm 122: 2

The Citadel of David

Street scene in Jerusalem

Walk about Zion, go round about her, number her towers, consider her ramparts, go through her citadels; that you may tell the next generation that this is God, our God for ever and ever.

Psalm 48: 12-14

Peace be within your walls and security within your towers.

Psalm 122: 7

Israel's future is assured. As long as there is a sun and moon

THE LORD WHO GIVES US SUNLIGHT IN THE DAYTIME AND THE MOON AND STARS TO LIGHT THE NIGHT, . . . – SAYS THIS:
I AM AS LIKELY TO REJECT MY PEOPLE ISRAEL AS I AM TO DO AWAY WITH THESE LAWS OF NATURE!
NOT UNTIL THE HEAVENS CAN BE MEASURED . . . WILL I CONSIDER CASTING THEM AWAY FOREVER FOR THEIR SINS!
JEREMIAH 31 v35v36v37

WHEN THE MESSIAH REIGNS, THERE WILL BE AN IDEAL UNITING OF THE NATIONS.
'It shall come to pass in the latter days that Jerusalem and the House of the Lord shall be established . . . All nations shall flow into it, and many people shall say, 'Let us go up to the mountain of the Lord , to the house of the God of Jacob . . . that we may walk in His paths.' He shall judge between the nations, and they shall beat their swords into plowshares and their spears into pruning hooks; nation shall not lift up sword against nation, neither shall they learn war any more.' Isaiah 2: 2-4

'Never again shall you be termed Forsaken, neither shall thy land any more be termed Desolate . . . for the Lord delights in thee.' Isaiah 62: 4

'Violence shall no more be heard in your land, devastation or destruction within your borders; you shall call your walls Salvation and your gates Praise.' Isaiah 60: 18

'Then the people of Judah and Israel will unite with one leader, they will return from exile together.' What a day that will be when God will save His people. *'The Lord thy God in the midst of thee is mighty; He will save, He will rejoice over Thee with joy, He will rest in His love, He will joy over thee with singing.'* Zephaniah 3: 17

'And they shall look on Him whom they pierced', and acknowledge the Lord Jesus as their Saviour and Redeemer. THEN 'the Lord will give them twice as many blessings as He gave them punishment before.' THEN 'the Lord will be KING over all the earth.'
'Who is a God like you who pardons the sins of the survivors, who retains not His anger forever because He delights in mercy and will cast our sins into the depths of the sea.' Micah 7: 18

'I will plant them upon their own land and they shall never again be plucked up out of the land which I have given them', says the Lord. Amos 9: 15

'The wolf shall dwell with the lamb, and the leopard shall lie down with the kid, and the calf and the lion and the fatling together, and a little child shall lead them, for the earth shall be full of the knowledge of the Lord as the waters cover the sea.' Isaiah 11: 6-9

Just as Israel's bondage in Egypt worsened before God's miraculous deliverance came, the Bible indicates that 'a time of Jacob's trouble' will precede the final and complete redemption. This troublesome time predicted, is spoken of as the 'Great Tribulation' and will be climaxed by 'Armageddon'. Jesus said of that period, *'that unless those days were shortened no human being would be saved.'* Matthew 24: 22

When defeat and annihilation seems inevitable for Israel, Messiah will place His feet on the mount of Olives. Zechariah 14: 4

*And He
shall reign
forever and ever
King of Kings
and
Lord of Lords*

Scripture Index

BS
630
C52

Clack, Clem, comp.
    The Bible in focus : a pictorial of prophecies
people and places / compiled by Clem Clack in
assoc. with Dawn Saward & Olive Clack. --
Victoria, Australia : Donors Inc., c1980.

20513

    160 p. : ill. ; 29 cm.
    Includes bibliography and indexes.
    ISBN 0-908250-00-2

    1. Bible--Geography. I. Saward, Dawn, joint
author. II. Clack, Olive, joint author.
III. Title.

ITALY

•Rome

Adriatic

Sea

Tyrrhennian

Sea

Siculi

GREECE

Aegean Sea

THE · GREAT SEA

EGYPT